Mindfulness Therapy

Free Your Mind From Stress, Anxiety and Depression

(The Essentials of Becoming a Mindful Person for Your Personal Growth)

Sidney Jerkins

Published by Rob Miles

© **Sidney Jerkins**

All Rights Reserved

Mindfulness Therapy: Free Your Mind From Stress, Anxiety and Depression (The Essentials of Becoming a Mindful Person for Your Personal Growth)

ISBN 978-1-989990-96-4

All rights reserved. No part of this guide may be reproduced in any form without permission in writing from the publisher except in the case of brief quotations embodied in critical articles or reviews.

Legal & Disclaimer

The information contained in this book is not designed to replace or take the place of any form of medicine or professional medical advice. The information in this book has been provided for educational and entertainment purposes only.

The information contained in this book has been compiled from sources deemed reliable, and it is accurate to the best of the Author's knowledge; however, the Author cannot guarantee its accuracy and validity and cannot be held liable for any errors or omissions. Changes are periodically made to this book. You must consult your doctor or get professional medical advice before using any of the suggested remedies, techniques, or information in this book.

Upon using the information contained in this book, you agree to hold harmless the Author from and against any damages, costs, and expenses, including any legal fees potentially resulting from the application of any of the information provided by this guide. This disclaimer applies to any damages or injury caused by the use and application, whether directly or indirectly, of any advice or information presented, whether for breach of contract, tort, negligence, personal injury, criminal intent, or under any other cause of action.

You agree to accept all risks of using the information presented inside this book. You need to consult a professional medical practitioner in order to ensure you are both able and healthy enough to participate in this program.

Table of Contents

INTRODUCTION 1

CHAPTER 1: GOING OVER THE HISTORY OF MINDFULNESS MEDITATION 5

CHAPTER 2: THE BASICS OF MINDFULNESS PRACTICE 20

CHAPTER 3: BENEFITS OF MINDFULNESS 27

CHAPTER 4: MEDITATION TECHNIQUE FOR BEGINNER 40

CHAPTER 5: MINDFULNESS MEDITATION 44

CHAPTER 6: MINDFUL ATTITUDES TO HELP OVERCOME ANXIETY 61

CHAPTER 7: PREPARATION TO MEDITATION: CULTIVATING ATTITUDES FOR MINDFULNESS 71

CHAPTER 8: MINDFULNESS TECHNIQUES 75

CHAPTER 9: MINDFUL AWARENESS EXERCISES 85

CHAPTER 10: USING COGNITIVE RESTRUCTURING IN REAL LIFE 90

CHAPTER 11: THE BENEFITS OF MEDITATION 101

CHAPTER 12: THE EMOTIONAL EMPATH 114

CHAPTER 13: MINDFULNESS TECHNIQUE #2: THE FREEZE FRAME 123

CHAPTER 14: MEDITATION TIPS FOR BEGINNERS. 131

CHAPTER 15: BOOSTING OVERALL CONCENTRATION 136

CHAPTER 16: RESPONDING VS REACTING 143

CHAPTER 17: KARMA AND VIPAKA 160

CHAPTER 18: AN HOUR OF SILENCE 175

CHAPTER 19: THE BEST WAY TO USE SELF-COMPASSION TO BEAT ANXIETY 179

CHAPTER 20: WALKING MEDITATION 195

CONCLUSION 204

Introduction

Do you think about the future often or do you have a tendency to dwell on the past? Do you often zone out or daydream? Do you often worry about things that don't even matter? Do you routinely relive an embarrassing memory?

It's a common knowledge that worrying is a symptom of an anxiety disorder. But, surprisingly, daydreaming is also a symptom of anxiety and depression. Thinking about the past or the future turns off some parts of your brain. This is the reason why you tend to forget things when you're worrying or day dreaming. Thinking about the future or the past too much can wreak havoc in your life. It can keep you from enjoying the little things and joys in life. It can keep you from noticing awesome everyday things. Worrying or daydreaming too often can make you feel like you are sleepwalking through life. Five to ten years from now, you wouldn't have any idea where your years went. Not living in the present moment can drain your energy. It also keeps you from catching key information. It reduces your productivity, compassion, and gratitude. It also stops you from living fully.

So, if you want to live a fulfilling and happy life, you have to enjoy every moment of it. Living in the moment can improve your life in many ways. It can:

Take the edge off and reduce physical pain.

It allows you to control your cravings and enjoy your food.

It gets things done so it improves your productivity.

It helps you learn new things.

It helps you appreciate the little things in life.

It improves your creativity.

It allows you to establish healthier and mutually respectful relationships.

It allows you to be connected with your surroundings and with life, in general.

It creates strong feelings of inner peace and strength.

It improves the level of your happiness.

This book contains tips and strategies that will help you practice mindfulness in your daily life. You'll learn how to practice mindfulness through meditation. You'll also learn how to incorporate mindfulness techniques in your daily tasks such as eating, walking, or even brushing your teeth. This book also answers frequently asked questions about mindfulness and contains tips that will help you jumpstart your meditation practice.

Mindfulness or living in the present moment can change your life on different levels. It can improve your relationships, your career, and even it can even expedite your personal growth. So, if you're feeling like life passes you by, it's time to take matters into your own hands and start living in the present moment. Soon, you'll see positive changes in your life. You'll be happier, more grounded, and more fulfilled. When you live in the present moment, the world becomes your playground.

Thanks again for downloading this book, I hope you enjoy it!

Chapter 1: Going Over The History Of Mindfulness Meditation

It is important that you know where mindfulness meditation comes from because, without this knowledge, you may question its origins and question why you should practice it in your life. If you were to practice hula-hoop every day of your life, the chances are that you would want to know that it was doing something good for your body and without that proof would probably put it aside after a short while. Comparing it with hula hoop may seem a little strange, but there are other actions that you do every day without question because your parents taught you that this was the right thing to do. For example, habits like cleaning your teeth or habits such as eating your dinner are all activities that you do because you know it's the right thing to do. You may not always eat the best things for your body because habits today mean that you eat mass-produced food and don't take much notice of what it's doing to your body.

However, the underlying reason you do these hobbies is obvious to you. Mindfulness meditation, on the other hand, at this moment, is simply an activity that has little meaning to you. Your parents didn't teach it to you, so it doesn't come naturally to you. Assuming that you are a grown-up, you thus need some form of proof that meditation works, and thus, the history is helpful to show you this and to demonstrate its worth. This is further backed up over the course of the book by helping you to become familiar with the scientific and medical viewpoint that has been formed by people who work in those industries and who believe in what they see on MRI scans and the behavior they have experienced through experimentation and investigation.

Eastern philosophy has embraced meditation for centuries, although the western world was a little late in catching onto its benefits. Practiced up to four centuries before the birth of Christ, meditation has been used as a practice whereby one is taught that by control of the mind, one can gain a better spiritual insight and live a better life. It is said that meditation is firmly rooted in Buddhism, but it can be traced further back in time to before the life of the original Buddha, because we know from historical accounts that the Buddha himself practiced and was taught meditation during the course of his education and thus it must have been in existence before he was born. This inner view of self was used to try to find philosophical answers to questions of great importance. Thus, many learned the ways of meditation and used it to get a better understanding of life. We have been asking for answers to life for all these generations, and today's generation is no different. The fact that our lives are masked by technology and advancement in medical science means that we now have ways in which to study the effectiveness of meditation and mindfulness that we never had before.

If we look into origins, the word "meditation" derives from the Latin word meditatum, and it is obvious why. The Latin original relates to pondering, and that's a good description of what meditation encompasses. There have been some thoughts by experts that meditation may have dated back as far as Neanderthal man. Although, the majority of studies on the subject find evidence that meditation started in countries such as India and China, where people were following the guidelines of religions such as Jainism, when Dhyāna or Jhāna, as well as Hindu practices, were common.

What has this to do with modern meditation and mindfulness?

The fact is there are many similarities between what is practiced today and what was practiced in those days. And that this practice has simply been updated to cater for people of the 21st century. Just as prayer takes on different forms over the centuries, so does meditation because the needs of people differ, and the stresses faced by humans also differ with the times. However, we can see from the enlightenment of the original Buddha that the benefits to be gained from meditation include the ability to see things in a clearer way and to decipher the codes of life in a manner that helps them to make a lot of sense. Our problems today may be very different to the problems of the times back then, but the fact is that meditation was used as a way for people to find answers to problems and although our problems may be different to those of people who came before us, they were certainly as real.

The ancient Chinese philosopher, Laozi, refers in scripts to the use of meditation during the 3rd to 6th century BC. And it's quite delightful to look back at the history of meditation and find descriptions of the practice that are in accord with modern descriptions of taking the middle way, or, as referred to in Buddhism, the Eightfold Path. We know, for example, that words like Shou Jing merely meant holding on to one's tranquility, while other phrases written by the philosopher such as bao yi described the behavior as embracing the one and bao pu as realizing the potential of simplicity. So who was "the one"? The one is the feeling of singularity, but it's also the feeling of completeness that you achieve when you meditate. You are at one with yourself and the world around you, and thus, the one is you — at that moment in time when meditation takes place.

The original Buddha was a Prince who lived in a protected environment, although when he was born, his father was told that his son would either become a great warrior or that he would become a spiritual leader. It was this prediction that led the King to educate his son in subjects such as meditation. And it was through this action that Prince Siddhartha Gautama came up with a clearer view as to what actions could help mankind to suffer less in their lives — which are the guidelines followed these days by the

Buddhist monks and those believing in Buddhism. Buddhism is, in fact, a philosophy rather than a religion. People don't worship the Buddha, but they look toward his statue for inspiration while meditating on life. The rules of the Buddhist philosophy are quite simple in nature, although complex to perform, basically, state that we must live by eight rules if we wish to lessen the effect of negativity in our lives and start to embrace life for what it offers. Mindfulness has encompassed many of these rules but in a modern way so that people today can understand and relate to them. The eightfold path is not something that is referred to when relating to Mindfulness Meditation, but it does form part of the history of meditation in that you are expected to live your life within certain parameters, which include the following elements:

Right Understanding Right thought

Right Speech

Right Action

Right Livelihood

Right Effort

Right Mindfulness

Right Concentration

You don't have to delve deeper into this philosophy to know that it is a timeless philosophy in that all of these actions relate to the behavior of human beings at any time, whether two centuries before the birth of Christ or during the 21st century. All of these paths were explained in an attempt to make human beings live more meaningful and happier, and we all have the power within us to control those things that affect our emotional response to life even though some of the above items could be interpreted in different ways by people looking for different solutions. For example, the right understanding could be widened to the understanding that the world is forever changing and that we need to accept the temporal effect of getting older. It could also be interpreted as understanding our mistakes and using them to advance in our lives and be used as lessons as opposed to being treated as negative experiences.

Similarly, you may wonder why your profession comes into the picture, but this also affects who you are. If you are in work that makes you unhappy and miserable, then the profession affects your approach to life, so including an item such as the right livelihood makes sense. If your profession embraces all that you believe in and is a vocation, then the chances of inner contentment are more apparent than when working for someone you know to be exploiting others. It all makes perfect sense when you relate each of the items in that list to your everyday life, and although this list was produced as a result of the meditation of the original Buddha so many years before the birth of Christ, each item has relevance to your life today. Does this matter to mindfulness? I believe it pays you to know what these items are so that you can appraise your own life and the part that it plays toward your stress levels, so yes, it's every bit as important these days as it is historically.

Meditation practices are common everyday principles in Buddhism, and the interesting thing is that the current Dalai Lama has been working with medical scientists and doctors to explain how Buddhism addresses certain social issues so that elements of Buddhism can be used in modern days to help people to lessen their level of stress. The Buddhist philosophy cannot be given all of the credit for modern-day Mindfulness Meditation, however, but there has been an investigation into why it helps people who suffer stress, and this has been backed up by science, as will be explained in the next chapter. The fact is though, that Buddhists already follow a path of mindfulness in the course of their day-to-day lives, and this has been one of the main reasons for the tranquility that you encounter when you visit Buddhist temples and see the monks during the course of their day-to-day actions. Mindfulness Meditation is an offshoot of that original approach, so it helps to know the approach from a historical viewpoint so that it gives better meaning to your practice of mindfulness in today's world.

Mindful meditation, however, came into practice through its founders in a stress-reduction center at Massachusetts University and was brought to light by Jon Kabat-Zin in the 1970s. Following this, in the 1990s, a cognitive course of treatment was devised by Mark Williams, Zindel Seagal, and John Teasdale, which used mindfulness as the basis for cognitive treatment for depression and stress-related ailments. There was little wonder that this came about since the western world was beginning to suffer from unrest in the light of the Vietnam War and also the aftermath of that period. People were looking for peace within their lives and were trying different ways to achieve that. Although the amount of stress that people suffered from during that time began to become a huge problem for health authorities and it was a natural progression that led experts into looking into more concrete ways of helping people to reduce stress within their lives.

There is much great literature from the past that supports what we know about the history of mindfulness meditation. For example, if we look into the history of India, we find that the teachings of the original Buddha were not written by him, and neither does he take credit for them. He merely passed on what he learned through meditation in order to spread the word so that people suffered less. However, there is literature that backs up that meditation was used as long ago as 5000 BCE in the form of wall art. The vandalism comes from this part of the world, but we also know that the Vedas, which are written texts dating back to 1500 BC, was merely an extension of stories that would have been passed from generation to generation before that time in the form of story-telling. Thus, the exact date that meditation started cannot be determined.

Even Chinese history covers the life of Confucius, an ancient philosopher who is still thought of as important today, and the practices that he taught were also based upon self-improvement and morality. We know that his work took place around the 6th Century BCE and that the roots of meditation were firmly established during this time.

This is by no means a full history, and those interested in history are advised to read further literature to open their minds to the potential of the practice and to see for themselves how extensive the history is and what brought it about. Why did people look inside themselves for answers to common problems? The fact is that humankind has always had a self-seeking curiosity, and philosophy and self-development have always played their part in the many eras of the past, though meditation was brought into the western world to try to find solutions to 20th-century problems and it succeeded to a certain degree. We also know that Yoga was starting to appear as an everyday activity during the '70s and that this also encompassed learning to meditate and to use that meditation to gain inner strength and oneness that is often associated with Mindfulness and Meditation.

Even today, in India and China, Tibet and other places in the world, meditation is practiced and Gurus such as Sahd Guru are passing on the art of meditation through huge meditation centers across Asia, the purpose of which is to help people to develop an inner understanding of themselves and how they fit into the world that surrounds them. I hope that readers of this book will investigate further because, as you do, it unfolds a fascinating story that reinforces just how powerful meditation is and what it represents to all parts of the world in the twenty-first century. The power of a practice that has indeed surpassed the test of time cannot be denied, and the purpose of writing this book was to help you to discover it in your life so that the history continues, and people benefit from the practice on a regular basis, even amid the chaos of our times.

There are many YouTube videos that show how Mindfulness Meditation is practiced worldwide and these are enjoyable voyages of discovery into how people deal with meditation as well as explaining all the breathing exercises that form part of meditation and that help people new to this approach to see for themselves that its long history is certainly giving a picture of success and that people worldwide are embracing the practice.

Chapter 2: The Basics Of Mindfulness Practice

Far too often, reading up on the basics of mindfulness ends up feeling like reading through an especially eccentrically written essay. Many people do not whittle down the basics of mindfulness well enough, and many people end up being put off.

This chapter will give a concise breakdown of the basics of mindfulness practice.

I: What Mindfulness is a special kind of attention characterized by attitudes of curiosity, openness, and acceptance. We take note of our feelings, our thoughts, physical sensations and perceptions of sense as we are experiencing them in the present moment. A wise man once described mindfulness as 'paying extraordinary attention to the ordinary.' It's an apt description.

II: Who Who can practice mindfulness? Well, anyone can. Even the most disadvantaged and underprivileged persons can. You do not have to be some guru or a proponent of Zen.

III: When You can practice mindfulness at any time. However, some times are better than others when it comes to practicing mindfulness. For instance, it will be very hard to empty yourself and focus on the present if you are in the middle of a very emotional time or when there are distractions all around.

IV: Where Just as there is no perfect time to practice mindfulness, there is no perfect place to practice the same. However, some places are easier to practice than others. A quiet, tranquil place will be better than a place full of distractions. However, you can be mindful anywhere, even on the subway.

V: How There are a couple of dimensions to consider when you are practicing mindfulness — (a) the type of attention required and (b) the degree of formality associated.

Let us expound on these:

The kind of attention

It is possible to focus our awareness almost like a laser beam so that we become immersed in taking note of small details or some perception. Alternatively, the attention that we give can be one that allows us to be aware of, but not focused on, whatever comes up. We maintain a level of detachment without necessarily being disinterested or unfocused.

This difference in attention is achieved quite easily via visual perception. We can stare at an object and dissect its properties with our vision, or we can stare at the same object but instead of being fixated on it; notice and take in things in our peripheral vision, which is the distinction between diffuse and concentrated awareness. It reflects the dual ways in which you can practice mindfulness.

Formality

Mindfulness can be done formally as well, through meditation, or informally, through everyday activities. Contrary to what most people think, there are many types of meditation. You do not have to sit in a half-lotus position with the window blinds down to 'meditate.' The truth is that you can meditate in just about any way. If you are the type that finds it hard to sit still or have a particularly active mind, walking meditation may be a good place to start. You could even invent your meditation type. The martial artist Joe Rogan, for instance, has his form of meditation called 'heavy bag' meditation, where he throws a punch and kick combinations at a heavy bag while remaining immersed in the process.

Informally, we can be aware of anything or whatever it is that we're thinking of, feeling, doing, sensing, Etc. We can 'notice our thoughts.' For instance, it's easy to track the thoughts in your head when you are stuck in traffic or while on a commute.

We can become aware of our actions, for instance, how it feels like to walk, stretch, shave, Etc. We can be aware of the physical embodiment of our emotions, for instance, what happens to your breathing when furious. We can pay attention to our senses, for instance, seeing the visual signs of the changing seasons, or noticing your fierce grip on the leather steering wheel.

Quite often, practitioners make the mistake of overly glorifying meditation, all while being dismissive of informal practice. But the thing is that ideally, we apply the concept of mindfulness both ways. An analogy of exercise perhaps explains it better: Exercising and hitting the gym helps us get faster, stronger, leaner and develop better endurance. However, it will be hard to make any actual progress if your routine also involves fast food and overeating. You will get farther (even if it will take a considerably longer time) by applying more informal forms of exercise like walking, taking the stairs all while eating healthy. Of course, the best results will come from combining formal and informal forms of exercise, depending on the day's circumstances.

V: Why Why should you practice mindfulness? What is the point? Well, mindfulness helps us to pay more attention to our experience throughout daily life. This practice allows you to have a clearer mind and more understanding of what's going on in your surroundings. It also gives you awareness to what is truly going on within your being, for example: how to decode what emotions you are feeling, and what you're needs and desires are. Every person needs to construct and articulate an answer that is unique to themselves and their circumstances.

Here are some general perks that are observable in most people:

Research has shown that mindfulness builds one's attention span. It lowers stress levels, boosts physical health, and boosts your immune system. If you are having psychological difficulties, mindfulness will provide some relief.

It allows a pause before we can react in ways that may be hurtful. It is also a great interruption device when dealing with various negative things.

It 'invites' us to live and experience our lives in a way that is more deliberate, direct and purposeful

It allows us to be present in life and, in so doing, enjoy the better moments of our lives even better

In general, it just feels way better compared to 'being stuck in our heads and alternate realities'

The following chapter will go in great depth and look at other benefits of practicing mindfulness to get you excited to want to try this amazing practice,

Chapter 3: Benefits Of Mindfulness

John 16:33; I have said these things to you, that in me you may have peace. In the world, you will have tribulation. But take heart; I have overcome the world."

•The development of mindfulness has roots in Buddhism, yet most religions incorporate some kind of prayer or meditation method that helps move your thoughts from your typical distractions toward a valuation for the moment and a bigger point of view on life.

Professor emeritus Jon Kabat-Zinn, founder and previous director of the Stress Reduction Clinic at the University of Massachusetts Medical Center, brought the act of mindfulness meditation into standard prescription and exhibited that rehearsing mindfulness can bring improvements in both physical and psychological symptoms just as positive changes in wellbeing, frames of mind, and practices.

7
1. Mindfulness improves well-being.

Expanding your ability for mindfulness bolsters numerous mentalities that add to a fulfilled life. Being mindful makes it simpler to enjoy the pleasures in life as they happen, helps you become completely occupied with exercises, and makes a more prominent ability to manage antagonistic occasions. By concentrating on the present time and place, numerous individuals who practice mindfulness find that they are more averse to become involved with stresses over the future or laments over the past, are less distracted with worries about progress and confidence and are better ready to form profound connections with others.

2. Mindfulness improves physical health.

In the event that more prominent habits aren't sufficient of a motivating force, researchers have found that mindfulness methods help improve physical wellbeing in various manners. Mindfulness can: help soothe pressure, treat coronary illness, lower pulse, diminish constant agony, improve rest, and lighten gastrointestinal troubles.

3. Mindfulness improves mental health.

As of late, psychotherapists have turned to mindfulness meditation as a significant component in the treatment of various issues, including discouragement, substance abuse, dietary problems, couples' contentions, tension issue, and obsessive-compulsive disorder.

4. Improves mood.

Mindfulness practice may decrease misery and uneasiness. One study found that mindfulness practice was as successful as antidepressants medication in averting a depression relapse.

5. Decreases stress and its consequences.

Mindfulness can prompt less exceptional pressure reactions. This has numerous medical advantages, for example, bringing down your blood pressure and reinforcing your immune system. It's a quick-paced society we live in, which adds to and compounds regular pressure. Figuring out how to control or limit the impacts of weight on body and brain is significant in general wellbeing and prosperity. Thus, it's reviving to realize that a review of 47 clinical trials found that mindfulness meditation projects show "little enhancements in stress/distress and the mental well-being segment of health-related quality of life." Another examination found that concentrating on the present through the act of mindfulness can diminish levels of cortisol, the stress hormone.

6. Improves coping with pain.

People with constant pain who practise mindfulness meditation report less serious pain and agony related pain. They are additionally progressively dynamic regardless of their pain. A huge number of individuals suffer chronic pain, some after a mishap that leaves them with a long haul weakening ailment, some because of post-traumatic stress syndrome (PTSD) after a serious injury during a combat deployment, others because of diagnosis with cancer. Managing chronic pain in a more beneficial manner is the focal point of a lot of current research. Without a doubt, the quest for and clinical preliminaries of options in contrast to medications to assist patients to cope with chronic pain keeps on picking up momentum. Mindfulness-based stressed reduction (MBSR), a treatment that consolidates mindfulness meditation and yoga, has been found to bring about significant enhancements in pains, well-being, anxiety and capacity to participate in everyday exercises.

7. Improves brain functions.

Practising mindfulness encourages build your capacity to focus and pay attention. After some time, this training can sharpen memory and improve mental performance.

8. Assists with weight management.

Some mindfulness strategies have been shown to decrease obesity and overheating. Overheating is an unpredictable phenomenon with a lot of factors and moving parts.

In any case, for the greater part of us, eating a lot frequently indicates a sort of mindlessness. We wind up eating more than we set out to or much more than we truly need to. Since eating is such a daily schedule and regular action, it's anything but difficult to just wind up doing it, as though we're on auto-pilot. Unfortunately, this automatic way to deal with eating makes it difficult to keep our best goals for wellbeing and weight reduction as a top priority.

As of late, a couple of specialists from Duke and Indiana State University found that teaching essential mindfulness methodologies to individuals who battled with their eating patterns brought about lower rates of problematic eating as well as a better outlook toward themselves and their eating behaviours.

9. Decreases loneliness in the Aging Population

Getting older has its difficulties, yet relationship can be profoundly fulfilling and specifically improving. For some more established grown-ups, in any case, loneliness because of the loss of a life partner or spouse can be aggravated when there are simultaneous medical or mental conditions or issues to manage. One study found that an 8-week mindfulness-based stress reduction (MBSR) program lessens loneliness and related pro-inflammatory gene expressions in more older adults.

10. Banish temporary negative emotions.

Sitting throughout the day at a work area or PC isn't useful for your general wellbeing and health. The regularly prescribed counsel to get up and move is well-established in research. An investigation surveying students' every day waking development based practices found a less flitting negative effect from development in light of mindfulness and recommended that consolidating mindfulness into day to day development may prompt better overall medical advantages.

11. Improve attention.

Scientists found out that concise meditation practice (four days) can prompt enhanced capacity to support attention. Different improvements from brief meditation training included working memory, executive functioning, visuospatial handling, decreases in nervousness and weakness, and expanded mindfulness.

12. Battle Off Depression

We've known for some time since mindfulness meditation can be useful for depression, particularly incessant recurring depression. There's a wonderful book considered The Mindful Way Through Depression that spreads out how to apply mindfulness standards and practice to cope better with mindfulness.

Yet a few scientists are starting to investigate how precisely the mindfulness benefits for depression truly work. They trust that by coming to a more refined comprehension of the neural mechanics of mindfulness, they will more likely apply it to a more extensive range of individuals who experience the ill effects of depression. According to the Bible, mindfulness gives us peace. John 14:27 Peace I leave with you; my peace I give to you. Not as the world gives do I give to you. Let not your hearts be troubled, neither let them be afraid.

The case for the advantages of mindfulness in depression only seems to be developing the more we learn.

13. It makes You Fall Asleep Faster

You've had a mercilessly long-upsetting day, you just got every one of the dishes washed and kids into bed, completed the process of responding to last-minute mail for work, and finally, you get the opportunity to sink into bed.

As you lay in bed attempting to get some rest, your mind besieges you with all manner of stresses and worries, from what time you should be at tomorrow's staff conference all the way to the plausibility of nuclear fallout and the finish of life on earth as we are probably aware of it.

Sleep psychologists call this state "Tired yet Wired." You're physically depleted, being as it may, as a result of an overactive personality, your body's natural desire to sleep gets stifled.

Indeed, there's an uplifting news from a group of analysts at USC and UCLA who found concise brief mindfulness intervention improved overall sleep quality and daytime exhaustion among their investigation members. Obviously, the investigation was done in an example of older adults, yet there's no reason to feel that these mindfulness benefits for sleep wouldn't sum up to any individual who experiences difficulty with their sleep. Particularly, their primary trouble is calming an overactive mind and getting to sleeping first.

14. Increased Focus and Concentration

In today's progressively occupied and distracted world, it's harder than at any other time to remain concentrated on what is important most and hold our attention there, regardless of whether it's work, relationships, or our studies.

The capacity to control and manage our attention is as powerful a skill as any other we have. What's more, fortunately, in the same way as other skills, it's profoundly trainable. We can instruct ourselves to keep up focus and concentrate, oppose procrastination, and to keep our most significant needs up front in our mind. The Bible even admonishes us, Colossians 3:2; Set your minds on things that are above, not on things that are on earth.

15. Be a Better Listener

Most of us know how significant effective communication is. What's more, odds are, we realize that being a good listener is an imperative part of building positive and strong relationships and communicating admirably with individuals. Particularly the individuals who have a significant impact in our lives; life partners, friends, employers, kids, companions, and so on.

In any case, regardless of the regular insight that being a good listener is significant, how to really do it or improve in that area can be somewhat a puzzle. Strikingly, analysts at the University of Minnesota have done some fundamental work on the job of care in powerful correspondence and listening abilities.

Their exploration recommends some mindfulness benefits for better communication and active listening skill by means of two sub-skills associated with mindfulness: depicting and watching.

At the end of the day, mindfulness encourages you to be a better listener (and in this manner, a good communicator) by teaching you to show signs of improvement by cautiously seeing what's happening in a discussion and articulating those perceptions.

Chapter 4: Meditation Technique For Beginner

The motivation behind why a great many people seek after the act of day by day contemplation is to mitigate their psyche and assemblage of the rigors of cutting edge life and ordinary anxiety. Individuals in these present day times need significant serenity and are looking for a feeling of clarity of things around them. With a specific end goal to stay away from the weights of the world weighing downward on them they hope to pick up this from interior instead of outer sources, for example, solution, TV or liquor.

There are exceptionally straightforward and simple reflection strategies for fledglings to learn without the time and cost of employing an individual yoga teacher. Most these just include basic activities, for example, centered breathing activities or listening to a compact disc while at home to guide you to a coveted reflective state. Once beat, one can then proceed onward to take in more propelled reflection strategies as they advance along their long lasting trip of contemplation.

Simple contemplation methods for apprentices:

Centered Breathing Exercises:

Considered one of the simpler contemplation strategies for amateurs who are beginning from the starting point. Numerous starting specialists accept strict contemplation position is essential, be that as it may it is endlessly over-evaluated. It is just critical that you are agreeable whether sitting in lotus, sitting easily in a seat, reclining or resting. With this activity, otherwise called pranayama, the specialist starts to inhale at an agreeable pace from the nose with eyes shut. Through a progression of timed breathe in and breathes out more than a brief time a reflective state can be come to with great core interest.

Guided Meditation:

Guided reflection is right now considered the most widely recognized of all contemplation procedures for amateurs because of its simplicity and adequacy. There are different styles and routines, however the guided bit of the contemplation is a reference to the aide you hear while you listen to a reflection disc. Regularly these album's will play extremely unwinding music, for example, hints of nature which help settle your psyche to set you up for reflection. The aide will identify with you and set the tone of reflection as they go promote into subtle element portraying different scenes and how to inhale as needs be. At long last, the aide will lead you into the coveted reflective state whether it is rest, objective accomplishment, association with your internal identity or some other reason.

As should be obvious these are simple contemplation procedures for apprentices to discover that go about as brilliant hopping off focuses to alleviate their regular anxiety. They help assemble a thoughtful establishment the same number of cutting edge reflection specialists concede despite everything they hone these strategies all the time.

Science has demonstrated that there are great deals of Meditation Techniques for Beginners in the same path there are a considerable measure of favorable circumstance that outcome from contemplation. Most think they would never figure out How to Meditate yet when they understand that Meditation for Beginners can prompt lessened stretch, wipe out and avert emotional instability, ailments and solution, they change their psyches and begin contemplating.

From an otherworldly perspective, the lines of correspondence in the middle of you and the all-inclusive personality is opened by reflection. So in the event that you need to figure out How to Meditate in light of the fact that you're after the physical and otherworldly advantages or on the grounds that you're charmed due to it, contemplation can truly be valuable to numerous.

Chapter 5: Mindfulness Meditation

What is Mindfulness Meditation?

A generally accepted definition of mindfulness meditation (mindfulness) is that of Jon Kabat-Zinn (1994): to act intentionally and pay close attention to internal(feelings, emotions, thoughts, states of mind) or external experiences of the present moment, without making value judgments.

Other, more specific definitions have been proposed. One of them is that of Ruth

Baer (2006), that mindfulness meditation has five components:

Observation of sensations, perceptions, thoughts and emotions.

Identification of these observations with words.

The non-reactivity to inner experience.

Non-judgment of experience (watching without condemning)

Jeopardizing the conscientious.

The concept was introduced in medicine and Western psychology by Kabat-Zinn. Using techniques based on the mechanisms of attention and incorporating certain practices of meditation, mindfulness meditation offers assistance to those who suffer from emotional problems or are facing the consequences of somatic diseases.

Initiated in the field of health by Kabat-Zinn for stress reduction (Mindfulness-Based Stress Reduction, MBSR), mindfulness is now structured to cognitive therapy for the prevention of depressive relapse (Mindfulness-Based Cognitive Therapy MBCT).

Today, this method is used in hospitals under various therapeutic programs, and is subject to regular clinical and scientific research.

Why is mindfulness different from other kinds of meditation?

Researchers usually classify all types of meditation, according to the way they focus attention, into two main categories:

Focused Attention and Open Monitoring. I would like to suggest a third type of meditation, which is named Effortless Presence.

-Focused attention meditation

This meditation requires focusing the attention on only one object during the meditation session. This object can either be the breath, a smell, visualization, part of the body, or simply an external object. As the meditator advances, their ability to maintain the flow of attention into the specific chosen object gets stronger, and all external distractions become less and less apparent and shorter-lived. Both the depth and steadiness of the practitioner's attention become extremely elevated and developed.

-Open monitoring meditation

Instead of shifting the practitioner's focus and attention to only one object, open monitoring meditation keeps the focusing open while monitoring all sorts of experiences without having any kind of judgmental feelings or attachment. All perceptions, whether they are internal (thoughts, emotions, memories) or external (sound, smell), are brought into awareness and observed for what they are. It is the actual operation of non-reactive monitoring of the things the meditator experiences from moment to moment. Examples include mindfulness meditation, and also some kinds of Taoist meditation.

Effortless Presence

This is when the attention is not focused on anything in specific, but reposes on itself—quiet, steady, empty and introverted. It can also be named the "Mandatory Awareness" or the "True Being".

This is actually the real reason behind all types of meditation. All traditional techniques of meditation realize that the object of focusing, and even the operating of monitoring, is only a means to teach the mind, so that effortless inner peace and a deeper state of consciousness can be achieved.

Eventually, both the object of the focus and the process itself are going to be left

behind, and the true inner self of the practitioner is going to get stronger and slowly appear, as "pure presence". In some types of techniques, this is the main focus from the beginning of the meditation. Examples are: the Self-Enquiry ("I am" meditation) by Ramana Maharishi and some kinds of Taoist meditation, as well as some kinds of Raja Yoga. Therefore, given this generic landscape of types of meditation, we can clearly see that mindfulness meditation is an Open Monitoring meditation (unlike any other technique that is more based on Focused Attention).

One of the most significant influencers for mindfulness meditation in the West is John Kabat-Zinn. His Mindfulness-Based Stress Reduction program (MBSR)—which he developed in the early 1980s at the University of Massachusetts Medical School—has been very effective and was used in many hospitals and health clinics throughout the past decades.

The method of mindfulness as it is taught in the West is very much simplified. It resembles the various important Buddhist concepts that were the main motivation behind the whole practice, as well as the practice of ethics, which was traditionally interconnected.

I consider myself to be an "old-school" practitioner when it comes to meditation. Yet, I am very open to the new methods of practicing meditation, and I see that whatever helps an individual start the practice is in itself good. Even in the most simplified ways possible, mindfulness can bring countless benefits for the human body and mind. So, what's the problem?

Positive thinking

Positive thinking can be an extraordinary tool in accomplishing our goals in life, but we still need to know how to use it effectively.

"Think positive!" How many times have you followed this advice without obtaining satisfactory results?

Like me, you know very well that to succeed in something, the first step is to believe this thing is possible. But in this case, how can we believe this when our common sense tells us quite the opposite?

The problem with traditional methods of positive thinking and conscious autosuggestion is that they mainly use our conscious mind, and they often neglect the power of our subconscious.

You need to learn how to use the full potential of this extraordinary tool that is within your reach!

The limits of conscious positive thinking

Despite its invaluable creative and beneficial power, positive thinking has limits, especially when it is only applied to our conscious mind. Misused, it may even be detrimental to our self-esteem!

Are you surprised? Then take knowledge of the extract below, which may shake your beliefs or at least change your mindset so completely that you will call into question your old ideas when you use the methods to get you to a positive goal.

However, before coming to the conclusion that positive thinking is ineffective, depriving yourself of an exceptional, essential tool in your life, please read the explanations and clarifications below first.

The ideas below are some of the most important ideas researchers have come up with on positive thinking:

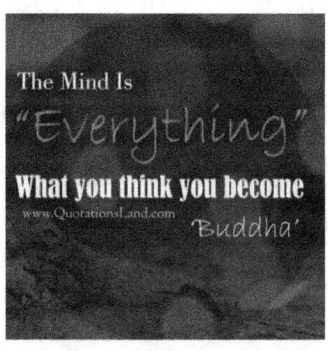

These conclusions are mainly based on a study conducted by Joanne Wood, a professor of psychology at the University of Waterloo in Ontario, Canada. In this study, Ms. Wood has examined the effects of positive thinking. It concludes that the positive messages people use to try to convince themselves can sometimes produce a negative effect, quite the opposite of what they hope for, particularly for those who have a poor underlying image of themselves. According to her, the positive messages work only if the person who utters them really believes they will work. She adds that it is paradoxically in people who have the greatest need that positive thinking will have a negative effect.

The moral of this story is that if you make conscious autosuggestion and this conscious assertion goes against your subconscious programming, you're not going to believe the suggestions, and if you do not believe in them, the technique will never work for you.

Fortunately, there is a solution for your positive thoughts, one that can give you amazing results, whether you believe it or not and whether your self-esteem is proverbial or entirely null. Moreover, numerous scientific studies have already proven this repeatedly.

But, before you discover all the ultra-efficient positive mental programming techniques, it is important to understand why strictly conscious positive thinking is not always profitable, in order to avoid the mistakes that will keep you perpetually in a mode of failure and disappointment.

Why is strictly conscious positive thinking not always very effective?

As the conscious only manages 10% of our mind, compared to our subconscious, which directs 90%; as these positive thoughts remain strictly conscious, we get only negligible results.

First, you must know that, as soon as conscious, positive thinking goes against our subconscious mind control, the mind considers it false and impertinent and, suddenly, it is systematically deleted. Remember that the subconscious is powerful than the conscious, so if you put them both in conflict, the subconscious will always trump the conscious.

For example, if you say "I have confidence in myself", but your unconscious's mental programming is different, your mind will take this statement for heresy; it will eliminate it and you will still be at the same point, devoid of confidence.

As if that was not enough, another drawback shows up when you use traditional conscious positive thinking:

since the conscious is the filter of the mind, any statement contrary to your beliefs is automatically captured and eliminated by it. So, any positive thinking you are unable to consciously believe will simply get rejected before even being considered by your mind.

Finally, as the conscious is the "**memory**" of the mind, without constantly asking for the maintenance of forced positive thoughts, it slows down its operation. Therefore, it loses effectiveness in accomplishing short-term tasks (logical reasoning, decision making, voluntary actions, etc.) which fall within the responsibility of our conscious mind.

Thus, if you should spend all day repeating to yourself mentally that you are growing thin, it will be very difficult for you to concentrate at work, calculate your budget, write a letter or initiate meaningful conversations with your friends, as you will be constantly interrupted in the course of your ideas.

In short, conscious positive thinking is not the perfect solution to achieve your goals. In fact, being virtually ineffective for some, it may even cause you failure after failure, decreasing each time your esteem and tapering your chances of success, as demonstrated by Joanne Wood's study, cited above.

Fortunately, there is a much more profitable method than conscious positive thinking, as you will see next.

The power of positive thinking or positive subconscious mental programming

So, here are the principles for using the power of positive thinking properly, so as to become the master of your own destiny...

To achieve tangible results in our goals in life, nothing equals the power of subconscious positive thinking, which we also call **"positive mental programming"**.

As we explained earlier, it is the subconscious that handles most of our mind. This operates automatically, without us having to intervene.

Consisting essentially of programs (like computer software), our subconscious is responsible for the vital functions of our body, so we do not have to make conscious mental effort to make our heart beat or to operate our lungs.

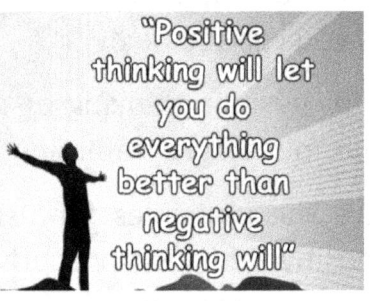

It is also responsible for the tasks we have to perform regularly, like walking, driving a car or brushing our teeth.

Imagine that every second of your life, you had to use your conscious mind to remind your heart to beat at the same time that you tell your lungs to breathe at the same time that you explain to each of your organs how to function and doing that while you were ordering each of your employees to move this or to do that this way or that way.

Do you really think that you could then remain effective in accomplishing your daily tasks?

Yet, that's exactly what you do when you abuse your conscious mind, trying to convince yourself constantly of something that you think is impossible: You then simply overload your conscious mind with information, and you prevent it from doing its job effectively.

If you want your positive thoughts to be profitable, you should instead turn them into automation by making the final pass on a subconscious level. In other words, your positive thoughts must become part of your subconscious mind control, so they can work in the background for you, round the clock, without you having to continually put in effort to make your mind aware of them.

Chapter 6: Mindful Attitudes To Help Overcome Anxiety

Once we learn how to control our attitudes and behaviors, then we will find it easy for us to cope with any situation and be kind to ourselves.

There are some attitudes which are very central to mindfulness, and once you foster these attitudes, you will be able to develop and then sustain mindfulness as a practice. Paying attention to these attitudes will help you sustain mindfulness in your life.

The following are some of the attitudes which will help you overcome stress mindfully:

Intention or volition- This forms the root attitude as it will play a great role in sustaining the rest of the attitudes. Your intention or the volition will give you energy and drive you towards working so as to overcome stress and live a peaceful life. It will also keep you focused towards attaining your goals despite challenges which might come your way.

Beginner's mind- You should have a mind which will help you see things from a very fresh perspective. Once you overcome stress via this way, your experience will be transformed greatly. With the willingness to adopt any new view which comes your way, you will have new possibilities and these will help you overcome any negative thoughts, feelings and stress in your life.

Patience- This attitude calls for fortitude and perseverance whenever you go through negative thoughts or when things get tough. Patience will also help you see times of stress as just a passing moment after which you will emerge stronger than you were before.

Acknowledgement- This attitude will help you meet your experience in the way in which it is. With this attitude, once you meet stress and anxiety, you will experience it in the form that it is instead of trying to just live with it. You will accept that stress is there and determine how much you dislike it. After applying patience, you will understand it is just a temporary moment after which you will come out victorious.

Non-striving- This refers to preparing you to meet any experience that comes your way and being ready to not change it. With this attitude, you will learn to accept what comes your way good or bad. You will also learn to accept the outcome of what you do, without rejecting it. However, you may think that non-striving will negate your intention to set wise goals and work towards achieving them, but this is not the case. With stress and anxiety, your aim will be to flee away from the situation. With non-striving, you will pause and try to learn something from the experience and you will not strive to exert any force into the experience. This will allow you to learn something new from the experience. With this, you will also become less fearful of the thoughts, emotions and physical sensations which usually come with stress and anxiety.

Nonjudgment- This means that you will go through your present moment without a judgmental mindset. Once you avoid the judgmental mindset, you will be in a position to see more clearly. If you avoid doing evaluations, the sources of stress will disappear. Whenever you feel stressed, adopt a nonjudgmental mindset and your mind will rest into a balanced state.

Self-reliance- This attitude will help you to build up your inner confidence. This is good for you to be able to trust yourself and turn toward stress and other uncomfortable feelings that you may experience. When this attitude is combined with the other attitudes of mindfulness, you will accept what has happened, and move on knowing that you are just going through a temporary moment in life.

Equanimity and Balance- These two attitudes will increase your wisdom and will give you a broad perspective so as to see things more clearly. From these, you will understand that no situation is permanent, and that your experience is wide and richer than any temporary experience of stress and other challenges.

Self-compassion- Research has found that most people in the world are their own adversaries. Most people find it difficult to treat other people in the same way that they treat themselves. With this attitude, you will make yourself your best friend even in times of hardship such as when stressed, and you will offer a hand whenever times of hardship come your way. This will also help you realize that you should always be there for yourself, and your stress will decrease naturally.

Allowing or Letting be- This quality is related to non-striving. It will help you give space to anything which happens instead of having to live under stress. An example is when you have lost your close relative or your loved ones. You will accept that it has happened without having to stress yourself about it. In this case, you will know that you had no control over the situation and move on with your life. Even if the stress was brought about by your fault or mistake, you will just accept it as it has happened, and know that what has been done cannot be undone. This calls for you to understand that you have a great future ahead instead of having to concentrate on the past events.

Getting into Practice

Now that you have chosen the best environment, chosen the best posture, set an alarm and assembled all that you will need during meditation, it is time for you to get into practice. The following tips will help you go through the meditation exercise successfully:

Beginning the Meditation

1.Relax the mind

You must have been thinking about a lot of things during your day. It will be good for you to relieve your mind from these thoughts. You might have been thinking about what happened to you during the day, maybe at school, at work or in your family. You may be stirred up or frustrated. It is advisable that you relax your mind and divert your attention from such thoughts before beginning to meditate. This will help you put all your attention on the present moment.

2.Take deep breaths

Deep inhalations and exhalations are key during meditation. Try to focus on the breaths that you make, right from inhalation to exhalation. This will also help you divert your attention from outside distractions, or even the past or future thoughts. Ensure that the breaths are deep, and focus on how you feel on the inside. You must feel good in the inside after inhalation. Hold your breath for some time before you can exhale, and then take a deep exhalation. Relax for a few seconds, while holding your breath to feel the full effect of this type of breathing.

3. Prevent your thoughts from carrying you

It is a common occurrence that one experiences negative thoughts during meditation. It will be beneficial for you to ignore such negative thoughts, and remember to focus on your breathing. Exercise more control on your thoughts. This calls for you to release any negative thoughts which come to your mind. Whenever you find yourself thinking negatively, divert your attention by identifying a new and positive thing which happened in the past, or which you expect to happen in the future. Most people give up when they encounter negative thoughts, but let this not be the case with you.

4. Return your focus to your breathing

Whenever noise and thoughts distract you, forget about them by concentrating on breathing. Breathing is the best way for you to divert your attention from thinking negatively. Do not judge yourself according to negative thoughts during meditation. If you do, you will make a poor judgment, and the result will be that you will give up. Before beginning to meditate, it is good for you to know that distractions are normal to anyone who is practicing meditation. The resulting strength will be determined by what you do or how you react to such thoughts.

5. Think about the present issues

This should be the main goal of doing mindfulness meditation. Of course, you will be anxious about the future, and be negative about what happened in the past. However, try to divert your attention away from these and focus on what is happening at the present time. You should note that the process of mindfulness meditation is driven by the body, and that is why you exercise control over the body. If you focus your thoughts about the present, you will harness all your energy towards handling the present issues and you will emerge a winner.

Chapter 7: Preparation To Meditation:

Cultivating Attitudes For Mindfulness

Learning mindfulness necessitates that you put your entire self into the process. It is therefore important that you have the right attitude towards this practice. Your attitude is the soil where you will cultivate your capacity to concentrate, calm your mind, see more clearly, and relax your body. Seven interconnected pillars of mindfulness help you naturally enhance this practice. They are as follows:

Beginner's mind

Patience

Determination

Non-striving

Self trust

Non-attachment

Acceptance

Having a Beginner's Mind means looking at any situation, no matter how familiar they are, as a whole new experience. It is looking at something as predictable as the sunrise, a breakfast cereal, the road going to work, or your daily meditation with fresh eyes every single day.

Patience is considered as a form of wisdom. It means being completely open to every moment, accepting its fullness, and understanding that things can only unfold in their own time. When you are bored or distracted while meditating, have patience as you allow your mind to eventually reach its desired state.

Determination is important here as well. When you are determined, you stick to the practice; you keep on going even when dark times come or every time you feel there seems little benefit flowing from it. You may hear teachers say, "You do not have to like it, just do it."

On the opposite end, being non-striving also plays an important role, particularly in the early days of a practice, when you seem to try too hard to make results. You can strive to lessen your thoughts, to feel the right way, to feel less anxious or depressed, or feel more relaxed. Setting up goals in a wanting or wishing way is simply counterproductive. When you are striving in a mindfulness practice, all you have to do is be aware of what is happening in your body (e.g. focus on a sensation) and return back to meditation.

As a result of all the above attitudes, you cultivate self-trust and the ability to let go and accept things as they are. It is about growing faith in your intuition or basic wisdom, and honoring your feelings and innate goodness.

Non-attachment is fundamental to mindfulness. Let go of the thought of how a friend treated you in the past, the fear of a future confrontation, the anticipated pleasure of a vacation. Similarly, let go of each breath and welcome the next one. Let go of any expectations of how your meditation will turn out today—if you will do well or badly or how you will feel at the end. With mindfulness, you learn how to deal with these experiences.

If you choose to let go, you arrive at acceptance. However, this does not mean accepting and not doing anything for a current unfavorable condition. It means accepting the truths of the present moment as it is. If you are lost in the streets, what you can do best is accept that truth first instead of rushing in all directions without a clear plan. Afterwards you can place your focus on getting out. Similarly, if you are too distracted during practice, acknowledge it first so you can begin doing appropriate measures to reestablish your meditation.

Chapter 8: Mindfulness Techniques

Stop

The mind lapses into one of its negative habit patterns, drawing us away from the opportunities of the moment. We go for a ride on the negative thought train. Because we identify with the negativity, we think this is who we are. When we become aware that our mind is wandering, we stop thinking and focus on our breath.

Breathe

Take a breath and gently bring the mind back to the reality of the moment. By simply becoming aware of our breath, we can stop the rambling mind and return to the present moments of our lives. This simple maneuver of using our breath to control the mind helps us develop our power of concentration. We develop single-minded consciousness by continually bringing our attention back to our breath, every time the mind wanders. With practice, we can stay increasingly in the present, bringing our mind out of its aimless spin, back into alignment with the present moment.

Present Moment

We give our full attention to each moment. We focus on the stillness within, the present moment without, and on what we are doing.

Frame

When we use the breath to calm the mind and place it in the present moment, we have an opportunity to choose from a variety of frames of reference for life, as it occurs. We cannot control most of what is going on outside, but we can control how we respond. We can choose frames that inspire, heal, soothe, purify, entertain, and transform. We can create any frame we wish.

Repeat

It takes years to bring the mind under control. Expect it to wander from the present moment into its old negative habit patterns. Do not frame this as success and failure, as this will cause frustration and tension. When you go for a ride on the train of thought and find yourself back in a lower state of consciousness, remain kind, compassionate, and gentle with yourself. Stop, breathe, and re-enter the moment with the frame of your choice.

One Continuous Sacred Ritual

With practice, we can become increasingly aware, awake, and attentive in each of the moments of our lives. As our will power and concentration increase, we can begin to string the moments together. By maintaining our focus on what we are doing at all times, we learn to stay in the present more and more, even when life gets rough. We see that we can remain in reality whether it turns good, bad, or ugly.

When we recognize that all we have are these moments, that there is nowhere else to go, we gain strength and peace. When our concentration is highly developed, we can stay in the present and maintain harmony and balance no matter what life does. All of our moments become part of one continuous ritual in response to the truth of life just as it is, with all of its sorrow, beauty, and joy.

When we bring the unruly mind under control through mindfulness, we gain access to the calm witness, the student in school, the actor in the movie, the servant of humanity, and the warrior who is ready for anything. The witness remains even-minded under all conditions. When difficult or painful, life is school. We enter our pain to extract the necessary lessons. When life is entertaining, it is like a movie or a sport. When we frame life as a movie, we are observing the show or acting in a role. This gives us some perspective and protection from over-involvement. Playing with life as though it is a sport or game lightens our burden. We do not take it so seriously. We are in service when we help others. We feel peace and joy. The warrior is ready for anything. The ritual transforms the ordinary and mundane to sacred and special. When we rotate these frames, life becomes one continuous sacred ritual, offering up its knowledge and lessons, entertainment and joy, and opportunities to love and serve.

SOME MISTAKES THAT CAUSE MINDFULNESS PRACTICE TO FAIL

There are many reasons why you might feel like your efforts to incorporate mindfulness into your life have not worked for you. Here are some common mistakes that interfere with successful mindfulness practice followed by effective ways to avoid and overcome these obstacles.

I do not have time.

People are busy these days. And, at first, many people feel that mindfulness is a waste of time and they should use the time to get stuff done. It does not take any time at all to practice being mindful while brushing teeth, taking a shower, eating or driving. It just takes a small commitment to doing it and something to remind you to do it. Yes, the sitting meditations do take time, anywhere from a few minutes to 15 or 20 minutes. In order for you to be willing to set aside the time, make sure you understand what the likely benefits will be.

I forgot.

It is not unusual to forget to practice mindfulness as the busyness of life takes over. Review the benefits you expect from mindfulness practice and make a commitment to practicing. Find a way to remind yourself to be mindful. Perhaps you can put a sticky note reminder on the bathroom mirror to be mindful while brushing your teeth, or on the refrigerator to eat mindfully. Set aside time on a regular basis and put it in your electronic planner with an alarm to remind you.

I can not stay focused

So why bother? It is perfectly normal for thoughts to wander. The goal is to notice those thoughts, dismiss them, and bring attention back to the mindfulness practice. Over and over again. It gets easier with practice but even skilled mindfulness practitioners must still do this.

I do not know how to do it right, so it will not help.

There is no one "right" way to practice mindfulness. Experiment and find the ways that work best for you and that you feel confident doing. Listen to a few different guided imagery CDs or attend a meditation class to get a sense of how to practice.

This does not work for me.

People often say, "I have tried this before and it does not work for me." There are so many different ways to practice mindfulness it is highly unlikely that there are not some that work for you. The only mindfulness technique many people have heard of is formal sitting meditation. They may have attempted to sit still for 20 minutes without thinking about anything and found this intolerable. That is good. There are many other options. Keep trying until you find some that suit you. Start small and work up.

I fell asleep.

You may find that you fall asleep when you meditate. If you are exhausted, sleep-deprived, and running on empty, it is no surprise that if you sit quietly for a few minutes and start to relax, you fall asleep. There are several ways to approach this. First, address why you are so tired and find ways to reduce your fatigue. This might include everything from improving your sleep hygiene to allowing yourself to take a nap. The second way to approach this is to accept that it is better to sleep; if you are that tired, then sleep is probably what you need most. This takes the pressure off and, as you address your sleep deficit, you gradually become more able to stay awake. The third approach is to make a commitment to staying awake while you meditate. Perhaps you could do a walking meditation instead of a sitting meditation so you do not fall asleep. Maybe you could choose a position that does not support sleeping such as kneeling or sitting on a chair with no back. Perhaps you can choose a time to meditate when you are not so tired.

I feel silly doing this.

Many people feel silly sitting, closing their eyes, and doing the mindfulness practice. Explore what feels silly about it for you and explore options for making yourself feel more comfortable. One option is to do it with a group. Another is to find a private place to practice so you avoid embarrassment or judgment. Typically, feeling silly goes away with practice.

It is boring.

Many people report that they feel bored when they first try to meditate. That is okay. Explore options for making your practice less boring. This might include trying a different mindfulness skill or finding an interesting focus for your attention. It may also include increasing your tolerance for boredom by shortening the time to a tolerable length and gradually increasing it as your tolerance improves. Moving or walking meditations tend to be more tolerable for people with ADHD or for those who feel bored or anxious just sitting still.

I do not see how this could possibly help me.

Review the benefits proven by the research that apply to you. Read up on how mindfulness works and how it helps your condition. Mindfulness has been shown to improve depression, anxiety, stress response, health, concentration, sleep, addictions and much more. Trust the process and give it a try before rejecting it out of hand. If you cannot do so, this may not yet be the time to incorporate mindfulness into your life. That is good. Everyone is on their own journey.

Chapter 9: Mindful Awareness Exercises

From the moment that you get up every morning, you do many of the things you need to do on auto pilot because they are learned habits. Mindfulness helps you to be aware of the functioning of the body and the way that the world works around you. In this chapter, there are some exercises to help you to let go and to concentrate on movement and awareness.

Walking Meditation

When you practice walking meditation, what you are doing is choosing a quiet moment in your busy day to step away from the noise of the world. You don't actually need a very large space to do this, but you start the practice by breathing deeply as I have previously instructed you. Then try to get the breathing in time with the movement of your feet. As you lift your left foot to step forward, inhale and then as you place it on the ground in front of you, exhale.

The awareness that you should have while practicing this type of meditation is of the mechanics of the body in time with your breathing. Thus you notice the foot leaving the floor. You notice how the muscles in your leg react. You notice the movement of your body in a forward direction. You notice the way that it makes you feel. What you don't notice are things such as:

- Worries of the day

- Thoughts about the next meeting

- Concerns about something someone said

- Worries about personal insecurities

You haven't yet learned what mindful meditation is all about so I don't expect you to understand entirely. However, once you start to do this kind of meditation in between awkward meetings or after something upsets you, you find that it stills the mind and allows you to digest whatever problems you have without even having to think about them. You are too busy concentrating on the breath and the movement of the body. Thus frees up your mind and that's a wonderful thing to do because your subconscious mind will find solutions to your problems if you give it the space to do so.

Mindfulness and relationships

It is quite likely that some of your stress happens as a result of overthinking things. When you are in relationships, it's very easy to get into arguments or to find yourself frustrated by the actions of others. Mindfulness teaches you that you are responsible for your own body and that you cannot be responsible for the actions of others, except of course in the case of children you are raising and trying to teach to become valuable members of society. You need to accept that all things change. Thus, when you feel anger, you are actually empowering yourself to feel stress. When you feel anything of a negative nature, you are fueling stress. You need to be able to look at situations without giving them too much judgment because it is the judgment that makes you angry or that makes you upset. Try active listening because this helps you a lot.

Let me give you an example. Someone calls you a name. If you retort with anger, you are validating what the other person has said. If you simply listen and let the moment pass, it is so unimportant that it cannot touch who you are or how you feel. You will see that this is as a result of weakness on the part of the person doing the name-calling. You need to realize that their activities are more a reflection of their own weaknesses and learn to be empathetic and compassionate. This means letting go of what has been said. No one can change it. It is something that has been said, but that moment has passed, as they always will. Part of the Buddhist philosophy is all about:

- Acting in the right way
- Being kind to others
- Being thoughtful about what you say
- Being aware and being compassionate

The way in which this helps you is that you are no longer touched by passing anger. Instead of retorting, you simply breathe. Let the words go over you and let them out of your mind. Be above anger and feel compassion instead. Whatever happens in your day, there will always be a negative side or a positive side. If you always think of the negative, you will live that negative. However, if you learn from it and the lesson is a positive one, then you move on with the right kind of attitude, so that it does not linger in your mind and diminish who you are. Remember, that every moment spent in retrospect is a moment wasted. Let go and move onto the next moment.

Chapter 10: Using Cognitive Restructuring In Real Life

So now you understand how to utilize mindfulness and you understand how to utilize cognitive restructuring. Ideally, you've also managed to presume how the two could be linked: we use mindfulness to recognize the negative thoughts, and after that, we use cognitive restructuring in order to alter them.

This has been utilized for some time now to treat things like fears, anxiety disorders, dependencies and a lot more.

But what if you don't possess any of those issues and you're entirely 'fine'? Well, in that instance, we can still utilize cognitive restructuring. Since the thing is, you can really use cognitive restructuring to enhance elements of your mind that aren't 'damaged'. Simply put, this isn't simply a method for healing but also a method for self-improvement. And there are numerous ways you can utilize it to make yourself more relaxed, more positive and more productive.

Also, there are lots of things that resemble cognitive restructuring but don't actually fall under the very same heading.

We'll be revisiting this idea more in future but for now, let's check out some alternative ways to manage your thought patterns and some different motives for doing it.

Fear Setting

Frequently we think of fear and anxiety as being temporary reactions to circumstances or provocations. But actually, our fear and anxiety could be much longer-term and impact our choices, goal setting and judgments.

Tim Ferriss offers a principle called 'fear setting' in his book The Four Hour Workweek as a method you can use to conquer your fears and therefore start obtaining what you desire out of life. Let's say you're thinking about finding a new job, making a career change so you can go traveling, or launching your very own business.

You've been considering undertaking these things for a long while but the issue is that you're too scared to do it since you think you'll that you'll wind up without work or without a loved one. Certainly, if you leave your existing job to go traveling, you wouldn't manage to get a job when you get back? And the longer you're jobless, the more unemployable you'll end up being.

Ultimately, your partner will end up being sick and tired of subsisting due to a foolish decision you made and they'll go away. Then your home will be repossessed. And after that, you'll wind up without a roof and alone.

That could all seem very over-the-top however this is the sort of thing we really think on a subconscious level at all times. And the reason we assume it is that people are naturally quite risk-averse. We developed in the wilderness where 'risk' would typically imply tigers. Because of this, we learned to become more reactive to risk and to protect our possessions more than we go after new resources.

But these days risk is quite rarely something life-threatening. Probably, risk will imply 'getting yelled at' but we blow it out of proportion since we're risk-averse individuals.

By now, you ought to ideally have the ability to guess what's following: though difficult, We're going to take these beliefs and fears and test them by checking out just how sensible they are. And Tim Ferriss' method is ideal for this.

So initially, consider what it is you wish to do and why you wish to do it. Now consider all the things that are currently holding you back from starting and trying. If we're referring to a career break, then your list of concerns and explanations might appear like this:

Presently's not a great time, you don't have a lot money

You don't wish to leave your partner for so long

You're scared your job won't be there as soon as you return

You're scared you won't manage to find subsequent work

You're worried that you might eventually wind up penniless, in the red or homeless

Now let's evaluate each of these ideas. To accomplish that, we're looking not just at how probable they are but likewise how you'd manage if they were to transpire. Think of backups and things you might do to hinder them from being probable.

Presently's not a great time, you don't have a lot of money

o There's never really a great time, and if you travel intelligently you don't require much cash o You might do the job online while you travel

o You really won't require that much cash

o Now is likely better than later

You don't wish to leave your partner for that long

o They very likely don't mind

o If it is crucial to you, then it's something you need to carry out

o It's advantageous to feeling spiteful toward your partner since they kept you from experiencing the world

You're scared your job won't be there as soon as you return

o It likely will be, go over it with your boss.

o Do you enjoy your work that much?

You're scared you won't manage to find subsequent work

o This is very unlikely. If you're competent then travel is going to just contribute to your CV

o You might even discover a new job and accept to begin later on

o If required, then you can get some part-time work or start a side business to give yourself some space

You're worried that you might eventually wind up penniless, in the red or homeless

o You can survive on savings a very long time

o You can make money in additional ways

o You likely have parents or buddies who would certainly take you in long before you went without a roof over your head

Now consider the alternative: do you wish never to go traveling? Do you wish to spend each single day stuck in that workplace without ever achieving the goals you wish to achieve? Let this inspire you more than the worry and now decide to break the ice.

The same method can help you to decide to begin a new career, to relocate to another country, or to undertake all the numerous other matters that you've been longing for.

Get Rid of the Fear and Date Anyone

So, in this instance, we've utilized thought challenging once more to break down our worries so that we are able to pursue whatever we desire in life.

However, another technique you can utilize is to recognize those fears as legitimate but simply discover a strategy that reduces the risk. In this part, we'll check out a technique you can utilize for dating that will certainly give you the self-assurance to approach and date any person.

So let's suggest that you're the typical awkward dude, for argument's sake. You visit bars routinely with friends wishing to 'pull' but you're too scared to move toward the people on the dance floor. Why? Due to the fact that you're concerned they'll decline you and you'll thus wind up feeling extremely awkward. That's a legitimate concern (even though we could question why it matters) so it's tough to refute it.

The simple answer? Reduce the risk and remove your possibility of failing.

To perform this, you can just evaluate the scenario before you approach anybody. So hang back far from the bar and chat with buddies. As you do, just check out the place for folks you're curious about and if you spot somebody, smile at them with eye contact. If they're intrigued, then you can guarantee they're going to smile in return. If they're definitely not interested? They'll likely just avert their gaze, and you'll know about it. But in both situations, you haven't lost face, and you can continue to hold your head high. There's very little to be scared of.

If they've smiled, however, then you can most likely relatively easily approach them. That doesn't indicate they're automatically into you, but it implies they at a minimum are available to the idea of chatting with you. So the following action is to go with your group of friends to speak with their group of friends. Don't talk to them only; talk to the entire group so you simply appear as someone welcoming, outgoing and captivating. Also, allow your friends mingle with their friends as well. When you get a minute, attempt to spend a little bit more time talking with the person you were originally curious about and who offered you the go-ahead to come over.

If the chat is going properly with the person you have an interest in, at that point, you can step it up one more degree by just offering to purchase them a drink. This is a very obvious sign that you're interested in them and so they likely won't say yes if they're interested in return. Now they're elsewhere. You can chat with them by themselves and evaluate the situation.

Lastly, ask if they wish to dance. And in case they say yes, utilize the same approach: dance increasingly more closely up until ultimately, you're totally sure it's fine to make a move.

In this scenario, you have now moved toward somebody attractive in a bar, but at no moment is there any risk of rejection. If they don't wish to speak with you, they won't smile. In case they aren't engaged when you drop in, they'll create excuses and you can chat with their friends. If they change their minds, they can deny the drink. If you're sending out the inappropriate signals, then they are able to deny the dance. But at no point have you humiliated yourself and you haven't carried out anything that you can't 'recover' from.

Consider other things that you're scared to undertake in your life, evaluate why it is you're scared, and then imagine ways you can navigate around that fear by staying clear of the worst-case scenarios!

Chapter 11: The Benefits Of Meditation

You have already read about the different aspects of helping you with stress and illness but what else does meditation do? In this chapter, you will learn about the difference in thought processes. You will also learn about how those changes affect your body and your approach to life and toward other people. One of the things that many people suffer from in this day and age is self-esteem issues. These are brought about because of the influences that other people have on an individual from a very early age. We try to please although sometimes, the route that we take doesn't please us much. We try to conform to society standards, but sometimes, that means that we measure ourselves against others, which is basically unhealthy.

Improved sleep patterns and more energy

Let's see how meditation helps you with this kind of dilemma or with the dilemma of being unhappy. If you are tired or not getting enough sleep, then you will not be at your best. The accumulation of a lifestyle that does not give you sufficient sleep is that people suffer from all kinds of bodily stresses. One of the best side effects of meditation is that you will find yourself sleeping more regularly and thus allowing all of the healing endorphins that make you feel good be released into your body. Have you ever woken up even more tired than you were when you went to bed? This is because your sleep cycle isn't responding in the way that it should. You may not be going through all of the different stages of sleep. During stage three of the sleep pattern, which is known as non REM sleep or the period when you do not produce rapid eye movements, you get a better quality of sleep. If you meditate on a regular basis, then you are likely to enjoy this period of sleep better because your mind will be accustomed to the relaxation of mindfulness meditation. In fact, there are several exercises that you can do at bedtime to help you to improve your sleep, until such time as your meditation helps you all on its own. I have detailed these in the practical part of the book, so that you can try them in the early days of learning mindfulness meditation.

Improved Memory

The improvement in your memory will be noticeable after you have been practicing mindful meditation for a while and this is essential in the kind of world we live in. Meditation clears the thought patterns in your mind and because of the breathing techniques that are employed, you will find that after each meditation session, you have the kind of clarity of mind that you may not have experienced for a long time. In a study done by the University of California, students were grouped into two groups, one who would practice mindful meditation and one group who would not. The idea was to measure which group was able to retain the most information. They were then tested to measure how the students measured small details and those who had meditated, albeit for a three month period, proved that their responses were more accurate than the responses of those who did not take part in the meditation process.

This isn't the only study involved. Kids were given the opportunity to be on a list without having mindfulness meditation, to partake in yoga and to be part of a 10-15 minutes a day meditation group. Those who meditated did better at remembering things than either of the two other groups. There is a reference at the end of the book that you can follow to back up these statements. However, when you learn to silence the mind, it follows that the mind is able to take in more information and use it more effectively than a mind that does not practice meditation or mindfulness.

Learning the power of empathy

One of the most important aspects of mindfulness meditation is that there is no judgment involved in it. I have said this before but I will repeat it because all of your life, you have had the freedom to judge. The fact of the matter is that it isn't a freedom. It's a liability and it tinges the way that we look at the world. When you learn to take judgment out of the picture, you learn to empathize with people and this makes you a stronger person. Empathy means being able to put yourself in the shoes of others and being able to see that there are more viewpoints in life than those narrow beliefs that you hold within your mind because of the way your life has progressed up until this time. When you meditate, you learn to let go of these misconceptions and see the world as a much bigger and more positive place. You embrace others and allow them into your life and that makes you a good ally to have.

The power to change your genetic makeup

You may think that's a pretty incredible claim, but I am going to back this up with scientific fact. The fact of the matter is that a team of researchers from different parts of the world including the United

States, Spain and France all came up with the same conclusion – that mindfulness meditation can actually change your molecular structure and gene level. Psychology today reported in December 2013 that what was observed between those taking up mindfulness meditation and those who did not was;

"Meditation was found to alter levels of gene-regulating machinery and reduced levels of pro-inflammatory genes, which in turn correlated with faster physical recovery from a stressful situation."

But what does this actually mean in terms of everyday practice of mindfulness meditation? There are certain regulatory pathways in the area of the brain. We already know that meditation helps those with inflammatory diseases to control their pain and to limit the damage done to the body by practicing regular meditation. Those who were regular meditators were able to perform tasks at random after the trial in a more effective way than those who did not meditate. There seems to be a link between the receptors in the brain that are known as pro inflammatory genes labeled RIPK2 and COX2 as well as a change in the HDAC genes that relate to cortisol release. If indeed meditation can do all this, what scientists have stated is that this reduces inflammation and allows the participants to react to new situations with a very energetic newness and lack of sluggishness that could be as a direct effect of these genes changing during meditation.

Pain relief

This has already been mentioned but how about this for an astounding bit of proof. In another scientific project to measure the effect of mindfulness meditation. This study took place in 2011. Bear in mind that scientists have only just started to take a look at the effect of meditation as a serious alternative to traditional medications. The idea was to place students who had learned mindfulness meditation onto a monitor in order to measure their pain levels when a heat patch was warmed up on their skin to what most people would find to be very uncomfortable. In the case in question, all students passed the test with flying colors and actually did not respond to pain in the expected way. This was done at the Wake Forest Baptist Medical center, and the guy who arranged the experiment, Fadel Zeidan, Ph.D., said that the study showed a reduction in the pain felt by the students who had studied for less than an hour a day and that's a huge amount. 57 percent of the participants also acknowledged that their level of pain discomfort was much lower than usual.

Scans were taken to measure the pain discomfort of the subjects and these scans showed an amazing level of efficiency, in that all participants experienced a reduction in pain and that this varied between 11 and 93 percent. That's huge! Activity in the area of the brain that works on pain was reduced to almost zero during the process of actual meditation. Having worked with students over the course of the last twenty years, I would add that most students do reach that level when pain is reduced and thus if you are a person who suffers from chronic pain inducing disorders, some comfort can be found by meditating on a daily basis.

Increased Mobility

It follows that if you feel less pain, you are more likely to be more active. Thus, meditation creates something very special in the way of help for those who are immobile through lack of exercise or because their illnesses keep them bedbound. As you can perform meditation even in the confines of your bedroom, this proved to help with mobility, in that those who practiced it were able to note less discomfort and more inclination toward exercising, even if that exercise only took them as far as their walking frame. It's not something that should be pushed on anyone who is suffering immobility, but it's certainly worthwhile trying because the system of breathing that is used is so effective that the muscles are able to gain sufficient oxygenation through that system of breathing and this helps to alleviate pain, where joints may have been stiff through the pain created causing the patient to stiffen the joint to try and relieve pain. That small amount of movement can help blood circulation and stop cramps from being an everyday thing.

Boosting the Immunity system

There are many people who suffer because their immune systems are impaired by disease or are not functioning correctly. Here, the Icahn School of Medicine at Mount Sinai got together with researchers from California to conduct tests on 94 women. What's interesting here is that none of the women had experience of meditation and half of the group were sent away for a six day retreat while the other half went through meditation for the six days. Before the experiment began, blood work was taken from all participants, which would be correlated with tests after the experiment and into the future to see how effectively changes happened. 20,000 genes were studied and changes were recorded. You can read the report in full here, but the genes that were of interest were the genes that produced telomerase activity. Scientists know that telomeres get shorter over the period of a lifetime, but that in those who meditated, they were shown as being longer. That's a pretty amazing thing to find because it shows that meditation helps to build up the immune system and stop the telomeres in their shrinking effect, which gives rise of many of those immune system failures. Another interesting fact was that those who meditated also had a higher level of amyloid-beta proteins at the beginning of the study, and this higher level could help scientists to understand why people who meditated suffered less from depression and anxiety. The higher levels were still present 10 months after the study, showing that the long term effects of meditation was certainly unquestionable.

Heart disease

Harvard Medical School is not the only medical school giving out advice about the benefits of meditation. In fact, the people at Harvard state that the way meditation affects the physiology is that t changes certain actions within the body, such as blood pressure and heartbeat rate. It reduces stress, which can contribute toward heart problems. Adrenaline levels are changed and cortisol levels reduced leading to stress. However, the Harvard Medical School also make it clear that healthy diet, sufficient sleep and exercise all contribute as well, so if these can be part of your everyday life, you may just live longer. Does it work on existing problems? Yes it does because the moment you introduce these changes, you cut down on the kind of stresses that encourage heart disease.

It has been said that mindfulness meditation can help you deal with many diseases. The chapter that you have read gives you examples, but I am certain that there are a million more examples of how they can help you to become a happier person and a healthier one. Remember your responsibility to self and use this responsibility to learn kindness to yourself and to perform your meditation on a daily basis.

Chapter 12: The Emotional Empath

One of the traits of being a human being is recognizing feelings and emotions in others and being able to empathize with how they feel. Being empathetic is part of being emotionally intelligent and a healthy way to bond with other human beings.

What Is an Empath?

Before we understand what an empath is, let's try and understand what the root word means. What is empathy? Empathy is the capability to share and understand another's emotions. Empathy is a genetic trait that is passed down from generation to generation. It is something that is automatic for some and far more difficult for others.

There is a small group of people in the world, however, who are born with the ability to be highly sensitive to the emotions of others. They are sometimes so sensitive that it is difficult for them to distinguish their own feelings from the feelings of others. These people are called empaths. Empaths have also been described as people who have the ability to psychically tune into the energy of a person, place or animal.

Empaths are generally the people that others seek out for advice as they are excellent listeners and will often make good counselors, therapists and psychologists.

Empaths are usually very creative and will tend to be very creative in all areas of their life, so you may find that an empath will have a very unique manner of dressing and fixing their hair. They may drive a very unique vehicle and their house may be the only one on the block that is painted bright blue instead of a muted beige or grey.

Empaths are natural experts at communication. They have the unique ability to understand and interpret body language, non-verbal signals and energy fields. Empaths will be able to understand the true meaning of the words people speak as well as being keenly aware of the words that people are choosing not to use. They are able to easily understand another person's logic.

As we have already discussed and will further discuss going forward, everything has an energy field and a specific vibration. Empaths are able to easily sense this energy and vibration. Many may not even realize that this is something that others cannot do because they have been able to do it from birth, so it seems completely natural to them.

While empaths are good at understanding communication, it must be understood that they are not necessarily loud or outgoing people. Some will be, if they have become good at shielding themselves while being surrounded by people. Others, who find it difficult to shield themselves, will be loners and seek to shut themselves away from society because this is easier than the onslaught of energy that they get when they have to engage with the outside world.

Empaths may find themselves continually drawn to nature. Nature has a grounding energy which helps them to recharge their spiritual batteries. Thus, it also stands to reason that empaths will be drawn to animals and animals will be drawn to them as they instinctually sense their high level of compassion.

One of the hallmarks of an empath is that they understand your point of view. Some empaths are able to feel the emotions of others without taking them on as their own, but the majority of empaths are emotional sponges which can become destructive for them as people.

Being an empath can be highly useful in order to truly understand and connect with people, but the high amount of sensitivity they display can also be a lure for those with nefarious intentions. This is not to say that empaths are naive, but it is difficult for them to understand that certain people are not genuine about the feelings they express. Further, if an empath is not practicing mindfulness or if they are constantly exposed to negative situations, it can result in an array of difficulties for that person, from overeating to addictions (Orloff, 2019).

The determination of whether being an empath is a gift or a curse comes down to the individual's experience and possibly also the environment into which they have been born. A man who is born into a highly masculine community where men are expected to be unemotional and stoic will probably find life in that community very difficult as an empath. Someone born into a nomadic lifestyle where spiritualism is embraced and not feared will likely find their journey as an empath to be easier as they will have the support and guidance they need from their peers.

Grounding

As an empath, it is necessary to be able to center and ground yourself in order to avoid being carried away by the emotional expressions of others. All of the practices discussed in Chapters 2 and 3 will be useful to empaths in grounding themselves.

Yoga is another excellent technique. The practice, which is now a popular form of exercise, has links to meditation and also includes breath control. Contrast therapy, which involves fifteen minutes in a sauna followed by five minutes in a cold bath, repeated as many times as possible, is a good grounding method to shift unwanted energy.

A cluttered, untidy space will be difficult for an empath to feel grounded within, so a good spring clean is one of the easiest methods of grounding. Spending time with animals is an excellent path to restore your intuition. Animals are always in their natural state and have no concept of emotional manipulation, so spending time around them is almost like a holiday for empaths.

Use food as medicine. Eat as many root vegetables as you can, as well as carbohydrates. Spend as much time as possible barefoot. The human notion of wearing shoes can interfere with our connection to the earth.

Technology blackouts are a good way to feel more grounded and less affected by the input of others (50 Ways to Ground Yourself as an Empath, n.d.)

Shielding

In conjunction with ensuring that, as an empath, you are grounded, it is just as important to ensure that you are shielding yourself from negative energies. The crux of this is that you are protecting yourself from the destructive energy that others around you may possess.

The easiest and most potent form of shielding is visualization. You should be able to visualize yourself as being surrounded by a protective white or pink light shield. Only positive energy can permeate this shield and negative energy bounces off it without coming near or harming you. This tool can be used anywhere and at any time and the more it is practiced the easier it becomes for you to visualize it into being.

Set energy boundaries at work and at home. A busy, stressful workplace can be energy-sapping for an empath. Create physical boundaries with photographs of your pets, surround yourself with potted plants or use earphones or earbuds to cut off the noise around you. Also, prevent work overload by regularly reflecting internally and understanding when you need to take a break. Schedule time away from people to recharge and do not allow yourself to be too tightly scheduled that you do not have time to recover from interactions with people whose emotional energy may be taxing to you (Orloff, 2019).

If you work with people, try not to have a home office where people meet with you. It would far better to meet people in a different space so that their energy does not remain within your safe space.

Chapter 13: Mindfulness Technique #2:

The Freeze Frame

Your mind normally works in a very uncontrolled way. I know this is kind of uncomfortable for most people. Most people would like to believe that they think in a very rational and orderly way. But if you are like 99.9% of all the people out there, your mind works like a runaway horse.

It works this way, when you pick up on random things that your senses perceive you fit these data points with how you normally choose to perceive things. You see, if you put two different people in the same room and you give them the same set of stimuli, their minds would fixate or focus on certain stimuli. These are two different sets that they would pick up on.

One person would tend to pick up on a certain set of stimuli, while another person would pick another set. However, they are given the same stimuli, except that they just choose to pick up on different things. This of course happens habitually. This is a product of our experience and our background.

Now, things get really interesting because after their minds choose to zero in on certain things, they then start judging these mental pictures. These are never neutral. Once you judge, it's like getting on a runaway horse, hang on to your dear life because the horse will have a mind of its own. It's just going to bolt and you need to hang on, or else you'll fall off.

There's really no point in trying to control a runaway horse because it's just going so fast and it's bucking wildly. That's how your mind works. The moment you get to the mental judgment phase all bets are off. This is why otherwise intelligent people who would like to imagine that they are very rational and reasonable in how they think often end up making the same mistakes over and over again.

It doesn't really matter what they've experienced and it doesn't really matter what they realize it for. As long as certain triggers take place and they perceive certain things, they end up behaving in a very predictable manner. This is "the runaway horse" effect. That's how your mind normally works.

As you could probably tell, once that horse is just bolting, jerking back and forth, and running really fast, it's not going to be very easy to control that horse. The good news is that you can control it with the proper skillset.

Just like it takes an expert jockey to ride a horse skillfully to victory in a race, you can ride your runaway horse in such a way that it leads you to a higher and higher level control. Of course, this high level of control is not going to happen overnight. You need to keep at it for an extended period of time. The more you do it, the better you get at it.

Mindfulness enables you to freeze the runaway horse

One powerful way you can take control over the runaway horse of your mind is through a mindfulness technique I call the "freeze frame". Read the process that I described above. It all begins with the mental pictures you perceive and the emotional triggers that you get.

By simply choosing to freeze the mental images that quickly flash in your mind as your body picks up on certain signals, you will be able to achieve a higher degree of stability. Of course, the first time you try this you're not going to take full control over the process. That's just not going to happen. However, by being more mindful of the images that seem to almost always get you upset and to lose control, you increase the likelihood that you would achieve a higher degree of control.

The reason for this is that when you freeze an image, you're no longer assuming that you've lost control. This is why the runaway horse effect is so powerful. When certain triggers appear, you engage in a non-thinking automatic process where you just assume that once certain triggers are there, there's really not much you can do about it.

You basically just give up. Well, with the freeze frame approach, you are given an objective opportunity to look at your mental images frame by frame. The more you hang on to each frame and freeze it in time, the more stability you get. You'd realize that a lot of the things that normally throw you off track are not worth the hassle.

In many cases, a lot of the things that you assume would automatically be upsetting are really quite neutral. If anything, this gives you quite a bit of time to objectively assess your mental images and this creates an opportunity for you not to get as worked up about them. The more you practice this, the less "emotional trigger happy" you get.

You would be able to distance yourself emotionally from mental images. Also, you gain a tremendous amount of control because you would be able to pick and choose the mental images that you choose to dwell on.

You see, your body is always picking up these images and your mind is habitually choosing which data points to focus on. With enough practice, you would be able to focus on data points that would not freak you out as much. After this point, you would then be able to look at the mental images and even learn the optimal way to respond.

This can lead to a tremendous breakthrough because instead of blindly reacting to things happening in your life, you would be in a position to deliberately control your response. This can unleash a tremendous amount of personal power because you can look ahead to the objective or end goal that you want to achieve and then tie your judgment of the mental images that your mind comes up with to that objective. In short, you can start living a purposeful and value-driven life, instead of just simply feeling that you don't have much control over your life.

You see, the external circumstances that you find yourself in cannot be chosen. That's just how things happen. However, you can always choose what you dwell on, how you interpret them, plus the emotional state that you get into.

With enough practice, you would be able to respond in an optimal way that leads to more favorable results regardless of what life throws at you. There will always be people who would be disagreeable. There would be haters, complainers, and whiners.

It really all depends on what you choose to do in response to these stimuli. Ultimately, they're all neutral. It really all boils down to a value judgment on your part. Isn't it time that you chose a more deliberate and purposeful judgment system instead of simply just reacting?

Chapter 14: Meditation Tips For Beginners.

Perhaps you have read other information online, or done some research and realized the huge benefits meditation has in our busy stressful lifestyles.

Technology and stress makes us lose our focus on what's important, and the chase for wealth makes us neglect our internal peace and harmony.

It is a wise decision investing in a course that teaches you deeper meditation techniques (see daily meditation Mindfulness Videos), but for now you and use these meditation tips for beginners top start on the road towards inner healing, emotional wellness, and peace with your life and also with those around you.

Practicing Meditation Often gives you Maximum Benefits in all areas of your life and it doesn't take much time either.

For now while applying meditation do so as often as you can to get the hang of it and later invest in the best program to learn meditation as well as meditation music and other resources that maximize Meditation benefits.

While learning you will find that meditation will nurture your consciousness, help relieve stresses harmonize the energies in your body for healing, renew energy and make you feel completely calm and peaceful.

"The Steps of Meditation Tips for Beginners."

A) Find a quiet and comfortable place to meditate where you know you will be undisturbed. You can use a soft carpet or firm cushion to sit on crossed legged if possible but this position is not vital.

B) **Close your eyes so that you can shut out the world and all external interferences. This allows you to direct attention to your inner self.** (Later once you have learnt more in depth meditation techniques, you can use other techniques of focused meditation where it is not necessary to close your eyes.)

C) Completely relax your body. If you are very stressed focus on each part of your body telling it to relax completely and then move on to the next. For example each foot, each leg etc. Give attention to what your inner thoughts are and see how they will start un-jumbling to give you meaning to each one.

D) Learn how to repeat the mantra of focus. One example of this is the 'Sanskrit Sloka, amaram hum madhuram hum'.

This mantra means "I am at one with the earth and nature completely immortal, I am bliss and peace", I am at harmony with energy; I communicate with the knower and giver of all things spiritual and tangible….

When you learn deeper methods of transcendental meditation you will find many mantras that can be used to focus energies. These focuses have been known to heal illnesses, relieve stress and much more.

E) Once you have completed your meditation ritual rub your hands briskly together and place them over your face to feel the warmth of the energy you have generated.

These meditation tips for beginners will enhance your feeling of well being, relieve your daily stresses and renew your energies. You will also be rather amazed to discover that solutions to problems suddenly become evident and clear, and stresses and pains like headaches will disappear as well.

Once you learn the infinite benefits of meditation using these meditation tips for beginners browse this website and invest in deep meditation training Videos provided daily for a harmonious and

fulfilled life!

'Everyone has a powerful mind which is neglected by the daily pressures of life and few people realize what can be achieved by rewiring your subconscious and training your

Chapter 15: Boosting Overall Concentration

Many people benefit from boosting their overall ability to concentrate, and improved concentration can be practically translated into many aspects of daily life. Concentration leads to success in business, school, or social settings, and with an improved ability to concentrate, you will find yourself far more able to accomplish your goals. You will become able to apply your mind in a much wider capacity, and distractions will lose their power over you.

Not everyone who is easily distracted has ADD or another attention disorder, but for those who do, boosting concentration can be immensely beneficial. It may be more difficult, and may take longer to produce tangible results, but anyone can benefit from boosting their concentration.

How does increasing concentration help in becoming successful?

Increased concentration allows you to keep your focus, which leads directly to success in any endeavor. Whether it's a new hobby, or a personal goal, you must be able to focus and concentrate in order to gain the requisite skills or experience. No matter what you choose to pursue, staying focused in both the short and long term is the only way to ensure success.

Being able to concentrate on daily tasks or activities will allow you to both set and meet your personal goals. As you decrease the time wasted or lost to procrastination, you will have more time for productivity and accomplishment. You will also gain more productive free time, without deadlines or tasks looming overhead. This increases positive, healthy rejuvenation in the long term.

Reading is a popular example of something that people have a hard time concentrating on. Being able to concentrate on an article will allow you to process more, read faster, and benefit more from having read the article in the first place. The same applies to typing, writing, or any concentration-heavy endeavor. All in all, you will be able to more quickly and effectively finish your work, and you will gain and retain more from the work in less time.

Concentration does not come at the expense of multi-tasking, in fact, boosting concentration can lead to an increase in multi-tasking productivity. If you can effectively focus on one activity, then you will have more energy to concentrate on multiple endeavors.

What is the best method for practically boosting concentration?

No one method has an advantage over others. In fact, any mindfulness technique leads to a natural boost in concentration. Learning to close yourself off to the external reality is one of the primary components of concentration, so practicing this ability in a mindfulness session will naturally carry itself it out while you are working on a project. For example, when you practice mindfulness of breathing, you are naturally learning to concentrate for a period of time on the physical act of respiration.

In that sense, learning to concentrate on the physical can be a good way to begin boosting concentration. If, in the instance of typing, you can focus on the physical sensation of typing, then you should find yourself more able to type without becoming distracted. Your thoughts will naturally follow the physical sensation of typing, that is, your thoughts will become transcribed the less that you are distracted by having to interact with both the thought and the keyboard.

What other ways will mindfulness help improve concentration?

In addition to increased productivity, boosting concentration also removes internal stressors. Emotional and mental instability prevents you from being able to concentrate on the task at hand, and will crowd your mind for the space required to hold important thoughts or to take action.

Reaching mental and emotional stability is necessary for positive, productive work. Calming down can be naturally encouraged by mindfulness, but in immediate instances, consider using a mindfulness technique to settle yourself in the moment. Choose any technique that you feel is most appropriate, and take the time to center yourself before embarking on a long period of work.

There are times when you may feel too unbalanced to work. Going out and practicing meditation and mindfulness in nature is critical during these times. Being in nature is incredibly stress relieving, and is soothing and calming for the mind and body. Stress blocks concentration, and can lead to anxiety or depressed states of being, which is why maintaining a balanced emotional wellbeing is critical. Do not wait for your emotional state to spiral out of control, rather, process and resolve everything through mindfulness.

As you gain understanding and ability, mindfulness sessions should become shorter, albeit more frequent.

Sessions become more effective and beneficial the longer you practice. Clearing your thoughts will naturally lead you into a session, and utilizing the different mindfulness techniques can help you to clear your mind or increase your focus in unique and effective ways.

Does practicing mindfulness regularly increase concentration?

As with any other exercise, the benefits of mindfulness often extend beyond their immediate applications. Concentration will come more and more naturally the longer you practice. Think of your mind like you would any other muscle: it can be strengthened, maintained, or wasted away. Moreover, concentration requires practice and determination of will, which ultimately leads to sharp and crystal-clear focus over time. Unlike medications, which have temporary effects, boosting your concentration is a permanent solution. If you do not experience tangible results right away, do not be discouraged. Building concentration takes time and effort, but the rewards are endless.

Chapter 16: Responding Vs Reacting

As you see, there are quite a few things you can do to help you respond to stress rather than react. This is a way to protect yourself because reacting will only cause more suffering.

You have seen that when you are under stress, feeling threatened, your brain is not functioning well.

So, in a nutshell, how do you respond instead of react?

The first step is to recognize. The first step in making things better is to leave the autopilot and recognize that you are under stress because if you don't recognize it you can't do anything and you'll just make suffering keep going. We have spoken about what happens physiologically under stress on the topic Recognizing Stress In The Body.

The next step is to learn how to work with the stress rather than fight it or running away from it. Fighting stress usually makes it worse. In order to work with stress and find a better solution you have to first go towards it or at least willing to be with it. We have spoken about this on the topics Acceptance and Neural Pathways for coming to your senses to detach from overthinking.

The one thing to remember from neuroscience or the cognitive science is that when you are sensing you cannot be thinking or building emotions. When you are sensing you are relatively free from making it worse. So the "Sensing Mode of Mind" is a way of working with difficulties.

As for the exercises you have learned to pay attention and use the senses in your daily routine, when you are eating, brushing the teeth, walking in the park, etc. You have learned the 3-minute Breathing Space, a Meditation Practice, and Mindful Movements.

Now, you will do one last exercise, which is the body scan.

Exercise – Body Scan

In the body scan you bring your awareness to the parts of your body, from the bottom to the top.

The body scan can be done when you are at home, when you are travelling, or when you are sitting waiting for someone or something, as long as you can stay still while you are doing it.

The best way to do it is at home, lying down. It is more effective, and the reason for that is because you're going to be inviting what is called a "Being Mode of Mind", rather than a "Doing Mode of Mind" and being is associated with lying down and letting go. The body gives you the signal of let go.

Guidance for Posture and Comfort

The practice is generally done in Shavasana (Resting Pose), so lie flat on your back and make yourself as comfortable as possible.

If you want you can put a pillow, or folded towel for the head, so the breath can be free in the throat and the neck can feel comfortable.

Arms alongside the body, just resting comfortably on the ground.

Palms facing up.

Legs stretched with feet slightly apart.

You can put a bolster or pillow under the knees. It brings a bit of ease to the lower back.

You should be warm and comfortable, maybe using a blanket.

You can put an eye pillow so you can be more focused on your body and avoid distractions.

You can move gently during the practice if you need, but you should try to stay as peaceful and quiet as possible.

Attitude

Invite to this practice a gentle attitude of it being a time for you. Time to support your efforts for wellbeing and health.

So as you settle for the practice, gently bring into mind some of the helpful attitudes that we talked about previously in this book. It is important to remember that there is no right or wrong way to do these practices, there's no particular outcome in mind.

You should just try to moderate any feelings of sleepiness and really focus in your body.

Allow the inhale to help you feel awake to this moment, so that you don't become too dreamy and the exhale can be softening and resting, so each breath cycle becomes a helpful aid to the practice.

The object of this practice is simply to notice what happens in your body, mind and feelings, and meet your experience just as it is. Every time you notice in your mind any judgements about not being right or not being good enough, you must remember that this is normal. I can't emphasize enough how natural this is. It is an inevitable part of the human condition. So when you notice these thoughts, just gently let go of them and come back to an open appreciation of your experience moment by moment. Invite the qualities of curiosity, openness, patience as best you can into the practice right now as you lie here.

Notice the body

In the spirit of looking after yourself, draw your attention to your body. Move gently into a sense of the body resting on the floor and notice the points of contact between your body and the ground. The heels, the back of the legs, the area around the tailbone, parts of the back, the shoulder blades, parts of the arms, and the back of the head. Bring the attention gently and clearly to these places where your body is supported. Sense the overall length of your body resting in this place. Sense if these places of contact are warm or cool, or any other tiny sensations of connection, contact, and pressure. Invite curiosity to these places.

The guidance of this practice will take you to the various parts of the body and you simply have to kindly bring your attention to these parts, just seeing what sensations you can directly feel in these places.

Notice the breath

Draw your attention to your breath and the breath movements in the chest and abdomen. The movements in the nose and the nostrils. Feel the way the breath flows in and out. Notice rise and fall, and allow the body to simply breathe as it wants to. There is no need to breathe deeply. Bring your awareness to the sensations caused by these movements. Take a minute to find a place that feels comfortable and clear. I'd like to suggest that this place could be like coming home. If you get lost, if you go on a daydream, or start to think about something else. Every time you wake up, you may come back to this place where the breath is. This is the anchor or home. The place to come back to.

Notice parts of the body

Left Foot

Move your attention down the body to the left foot. As best you can, notice any sensations in the toes, from the big toe to the small toe and the gaps between the toes. Notice the very tiny sensations, or the very ordinary sensations of socks against the skin, or general sense of temperature, or shape. Don't look for anything special or big. Just see what's there in this moment as you breathe in and breathe out.

Move your attention to the sole of the left foot and do the same thing here. Just take a moment to notice.

Move to the top of the left foot. Maybe feeling cooler or warmer than the sole of the foot. Check out the skin, the sense of the bones within the foot. And if, perhaps, there's hardly any sensation or no sensations here, that's fine.

Left Leg

Move to the ankle area. All around the ankle of the left foot. Again, feel the sensation of the breath and bring your awareness to this part of the body, the ankle joint.

Move your attention clearly into the lower part of the left leg. The calf muscle, the shin bone. Sense the connection with the floor as best you can, not thinking about it but just acknowledging the tiny sensations that might be there. The warmth or coolness, tingling, the texture, and sensations of the cloth against the skin. These are your direct experiences, as you breathe in and out.

Move to the knee. The knee joint on the left leg. The back of the knee, which might feel cooler or warmer.

Move to the upper part of the left leg, the thigh, the hamstring, this group of muscles. Right the way up to the hip joint on the left side of the body. Invite your attention to the shape, temperature, the feeling of clothing or blanket. As you breathe in and breathe out gently and clearly bring your attention to this place, the left hip.

If you begin to notice the mind is drifting, dreaming, or going on some other journey, if you notice thoughts arising, again this is completely natural. This is what the mind does best and the practice invites you to know when this is happening, to notice any judgements around that. Gently come back, moving to the anchor point of the breath. Feel settled with the breath.

Bring your attention back into the part of the body that you are looking at, the left hip. Not struggling with this. Just gently, in a good way bring your attention here. Be open to your experience in this moment.

Right Foot

With the next outward breath, move your attention gently across the body down into the right leg and all the way down to the toes on the right side, back into this experience but this time in the right foot.

Acknowledge the sensations from the big toe to the little toe, and in between the toes. Explore the sensations. They might be quite tiny, almost silent sensations.

Move to the sole of the right foot, and then to the top of the right foot. Move your attention gently, arriving at the ankle. The whole region of the ankle of the right foot. Feel the touch of socks or blanket. Sense the complex ankle joint inside.

Right Leg

Move up into the lower part of the right leg, the calf muscle and the shin bone. Breathe in, notice this part of your body. Breathe out, open to what is there in this breath moment.

Move to the knee joint on the right leg and the thigh on the right leg, up to the right hip. Each time you wake up to having dreamed off or drifted off, just congratulate yourself for noticing that you've woken up to this and gently bring your attention back into the body, back into this moment. Feel the breath a bit more clearly at the anchor place.

Before living the right leg and the legs generally, you might like to try, just for a moment, imagining your breath could flow down to the body and into the legs, as if the legs were hollow and the breath could go easily down through them, to the toes and then out again. Breathe in, allowing your breath to be natural. Breathe into the legs and out of the legs. Your legs are just resting in this moment, alive to the sensations in your body.

Pelvic Area

As you next breathe out, leave the legs and move into the back of the pelvic area where the body rests on the floor or bed. Bring your awareness to the whole pelvic area. The bone itself curving round, the wings of the pelvic cuddle, and a whole sense of the soft organs nestled within.

Back

Move to the lower back and remember that, if there is any discomfort - emotional or physical - you can move to the breath as a place of refuge for a while. If there is pain, just notice the sensations within it. With this in mind, move up the back slowly, feeling the connection with the ground.

Front

Move your awareness round to the front body. From the collarbones at the top of the torso to the ribs, and then go down to the abdomen, all the way down to the pelvic area again. Notice the breath moving in the body, the heartbeat, whatever that arises into your awareness.

Just like you did with the legs, you can imagine, as you breathe in, the breath flowing into the torso, like it was a balloon filling up with the inhale and emptying away with the exhale. Feel the whole of the torso at rest in this moment. Just feel this as best you can and gently bring your attention back each time it drifts off.

Hands

With the next outward breath leave the torso and, as you breathe in, move your attention down the arms to hands, fingers, and thumbs. Sense the hands at the sides of the body, just resting on the ground. Sense the warmth or coolness in the palms and fingertips. Bring yourself as close as you can into these sensations in this moment.

Arms

Move your attention to the wrists, lower arms, elbows, and upper arms, armpits and shoulders. Sense the whole left arm. Sense the whole right arm. Notice whatever sensations that are arising into your awareness - warmth, tingling, touch of clothing. Sense the breath.

At this point you could imagine the breath flowing into the arms, as if the arms too were hollow and the breath could flow in and down the arms to the fingers and then back out again.

If the mind is going off, drifting, or dreaming, wake up to this and, gently, come back into this moment, into these sensations. Just do this as best you can, without any struggle. Open to your experience as it is.

Head

With the next outward breath leave the arms and invite your awareness to the neck and throat and the way the head rests on the ground. Feel the connection with the ground or pillow. Sense the whole area of the scalp. Whether it feels warm, cool or maybe a sensation there's no words for, but you can still move into it gently.

Move to the ears and the jaw. Notice whether the teeth are clenched or not, whether the lips feel tight or puffy. Whether the mouth feels dry or damp. There's no need to change anything at all. Simply meet your experience just as it is.

Feel the experience around the cheeks, the nostrils, maybe of the air flowing in cool, flying out slightly warmer. Just check this out for yourself and experience the sensations as you breathe through the nostrils.

Feel the whole experience around the eyes or the tiny muscles and the skin around the eyes, and the forehead.

Having travelled right through the body with this open interest, you can now imagine your breath moving into the whole body, flowing into the whole space of the head, down to the torso, to the arms, to the legs, and feet. Feel the breath moving to the whole shape of the body. As you breathe, allow your experience to be just what it is, even if it's full of thoughts, or concerns, or body pain. See if it's possible to meet whatever your experience is and allow yourself to be just as you are in this moment.

Moving now into the transition out of the practice you might like to slightly deepen the inward breath, not too much, without strain in the ribs. Just to feel a slight stretch in the ribs and back. And with the outward breath, a long releasing breath, feeling the body soften. Repeat this a few times to feel the body stretching a little and releasing a little.

Begin to give your body gentle stretches. Take great care to move your body with kindness and awareness at the end of this practice, and take your time to move softly.

If you have already learned how to do the body scan and have started to practice it with your eyes closed, when you finish it, gently prepare yourself to come back to your awareness. Gently roll to your right side and press the left palm on the floor to help you rise without strain, so you can look after your back. Come to a sitting posture. Smoothly open your eyes, look to the ground, and then look in front.

Chapter 17: Karma And Vipaka

A common "law" of life which you may be aware of is karma. Karma means what you sow you shall reap, or what you put into the world will always come back to you. On the other hand, there is vipaka, which is essentially the maturation of karma: it is when karma comes back to serve you what you have handed out. These are two very important things to consider in life, especially as you are journeying into a mindful existence.

When you are thinking about karma, you should understand that it is a basic law of life. When you put something out into the world, it is inevitable that you will get it back in some way, shape or form. For example, if you wish ill health on someone else, it is inevitable that yourself or someone you care deeply about will be affected by ill health. When that ill health comes to fruition in your own life, you will be facing vipaka. In other words, you will be facing the reality of the karma you have earned for yourself.

Karma and vipaka are not cause-and-effect in the sense of physical reactions and situations. If you rip the top off of a plant and it dies, that is not karma and vipaka. Karma and vipaka are pertaining to what you experience in your mind and the direct reactions or consequences of your actions in life based on how they affect you personally. Karma is something you cannot avoid, and you cannot escape. You **will** face the vipaka of your karma one day, one way or another.

In Buddhism, there is a common lesson taught around karma that makes it easier to understand. This lesson makes it easy for you to see why karma is important and how vipaka plays into it. When you understand the karma of your actions and learn that karma is inevitable, it makes it easier to become more mindful over what you are doing in your life.

" When a bird is alive, it eats ants. When the bird dies, ants eat the bird. Time and circumstances can change at any time. Don't devalue or hurt anyone in life. You may be powerful today. But, remember, time is more

powerful than you are! One tree makes a million match sticks, but it only takes one matchstick to burn a million trees. So, be good and do good."

 - **Buddha**

This is a powerful quote that can really lead you to think about how life works. Karma is inevitable and it comes from every single action you take in life. Knowing that, karma can be positive or it can be negative. You can infuse the world with your positivity and have positive karma as a result and therefore positive vipaka will inevitably come to fruition in the future. Or, you can infuse the world with negativity and carry negative karma as a result, which means that when your karma ripens and vipaka happens, you will have negative situations come into fruition. One reality that you should consider is that there will always be both karmas present in your life. You will never be able to fully distinguish the negative karma. However, you can become mindful over how you view the vipaka of the karma and what response you choose as a result.

When you manage to understand karma and use it to your advantage, you can start learning how to increase the positive energy flow in your life. Although you cannot dissolve the negative, you can reduce how much it affects outcome you and therefore have a more positive in the long run. Additionally, you can

recognize negative vipaka and use it to create positive karma in the future so long as you are truly mindful and intentional about how you respond to the situation.

What Causes Karma?

The primary cause of karma is ignorance. When you are unaware of how things truly are, you tend to create circumstances that warrant karma. Greed and craving what you desire is another situation that can cause karma, as there are many individuals who will do illwilled things to fulfill their greedy cravings. In karma, the door is volition, which essentially means will. When you willfully do something without considering the outcomes, you run the chance of having greater karma. Alternatively, there is feeling which represents the vipaka. This is when you feel the result of your karma as it plays out full circle.

Are There Different Types of Karma?

You may be surprised to note that there are many types of karma that you may carry with you in life. These karmas each have their own cause and often their own outcome. They are ones that can be harvested for many years or ones that can be easily let go of. That itself is largely based off of the person who is carrying the karma and what they to in order to deal with said karma. The different types of karma are reproductive karma, supportive karma, obstructive or counteractive karma, destructive karma, weighty karma, proximate or death-proximate karma, habitual karma, and reserve or cumulative karma. Additionally, there are immediately effective karma, subsequently effective karma, indefinitely effective karma, and defunct or ineffective karma. All of these different types of karma are important to understand as each can affect you in a different way.

Reproductive Karma

Believe it or not, every single birth of a being into this world is affected by karma. The karma you carry at birth is based on the karma that was never brought to maturity at death in your past life. Therefore, you will be carrying that karma with you in your current life, good or bad. When you die, it is considered to be only a temporary end for a temporary phenomenon in the Buddhist teachings. Buddhists believe in reincarnation, meaning that you can carry karma with you for several lifetimes before it finally reaches maturity and comes to fruition. As a result, you can end up experiencing things that may seem "unfair" to you in this lifetime, because you are carrying that from a past life experience. The last thought you have in your past life before death is the thought that will determine the state you are in when you are birthed into your next life.

Supportive Karma

This type of karma is one that supports the reproductive karma. It is neither bad nor good in nature, and it is persistent through your entire lifetime. From the moment you are conceived until the moment you die, you will have supportive karma in your life. If you have moral supportive karma, you will be assisted in good health, wealth, happiness and everything else that will fulfill and enrich your life and assist in bringing you joy and contentment. However, if you have immoral supportive karma, you will be assisted in receiving pain, sorrow, misery and more. The supportive karma which you carry is one that you carry based off of what your reproductive karma is. Therefore, if you carry a positive reproductive karma, you will carry a moral supportive karma. However, if you carry a negative reproductive karma, you will then carry an immoral supportive karma.

Obstructive or Counteractive Karma

This karma tends to weaken, interrupt and disassemble the fruition of reproductive karma. For example, let's say you were born with good reproductive karma, you may be subject to experiencing various ailments and such that would prevent you from enjoying all of the wonderful results of your great actions in this lifetime. Alternatively, if you were someone who was born with bad reproductive karma and yet you lead a life full of wealth, joy, and peace, despite your negative actions in your lifetime, then that would also be the presence of obstructive or counteractive karma. This type of karma can completely switch what outcome you have from the karma in your lifetime.

Destructive Karma

The law of karma states that the powerful energy associated with reproductive karma may be eliminated if there were a powerful opposing karma from the past. This karma may be seeking the opportunity to operate and therefore finds it's window of opportunity and comes to fruition. As a result, it can not only obstruct but completely destroy the entire force of the existing karma. When you experience destructive karma, it could present as either a bad karma or a good karma.

An example of destructive karma would be if you were someone with good reproductive karma leading a good life with moral supportive karma and you then decided to kill someone out of greed or anger. As a result, you could be faced with destructive karma that would completely destroy your good karma and turn everything around for you, not only in this lifetime but potentially in many subsequent lifetimes as well. Alternatively, if you were someone with inherently bad karma and immoral supportive karma but you did something extremely positive and good, you could wind up experience destructive karma in a sense that it obstructs and destroys all of your negative karma and turns you around to have only good karma and moral supportive karma from that point on. You may continue experiencing this good karma for many lifetimes to come, as well.

Weighty Karma

When you are carrying weighty karma, it is serious. As with the previous karmas, it can be either good or bad. This karma produces results quickly, either in this life or in the next life. If you were to carry good weighty karma, for example, you would likely experience ecstasy and joy in your life as a result. Alternatively, if you were to experience immoral weighty karma, you would quickly be faced with unwanted and negative consequences that you would have to pay as a result of your actions.

Proximate or Death-Proximate Karma

This is the dying-thought-karma. It is the one that sets the tone for your reproductive karma. Proximate or death-proximate karma relates to what you do or remember immediately before you die. This karma has a powerful ability to contribute to what you will experience in your next life, and as a result, there are many traditions around this in Buddhist countries. In these countries, they often remind dying individuals of the good deeds they have done and encouraging them to do good acts on their death bed to ensure that they are blessed with the good reproductive karma in their next life.

Knowing this, a bad person has the ability to die with happy final thoughts and therefore be born with good reproductive karma. Alternatively, a good person may die unhappily or with a sudden final memory of something evil they have done in the past, and therefore they will be born with bad reproductive karma in the next life. It is important to understand this type of karma and therefore become mindful of your thoughts, then, to ensure a good reproductive karma and moral supportive karma in your next life.

Habitual Karma

When you experience experiencing karma for habitual karma, you are

the things you do without recognizing you are doing it. Habits are often second nature to people, and frequently become a part of their character as a person. If one is not being mindful, they may find that they fall into their habitual mindset, which can lead to ignorance. Habitual karma is something you experience when you fall into habit and do something that is normal for you at the right or wrong time, essentially.

Reserve or Cumulative Karma

All actions that do not fall into any of the previously discussed karma bodies are ones that fall into reserve or cumulative karma. These are essentially a reserve fund or savings account of karma for a particular being. As with other karmas, they will inevitably be dealt in one lifetime or another. Just like with previous karmas, this one has the ability to be affected by obstructive or destructive karma, and thus an individual may not experience the outcome of their karmic reserves.

Immediately Effective Karma

When you experience immediately effective karma, it means that you experience the karmic outcome in this lifetime. Immediately effective karma may be experienced, for example, if you were to wish ill-health on someone you did not like and then you yourself contracted ill health in this lifetime. You may even contract the exact type of ill-health or ill-will that you wished upon someone else.

Subsequently Effective Karma

When you experience something in your next life, this is called subsequent karma. It is karma that you earn in this life that you experience in the next life. An example may be if you were to do something extremely kind for someone, and then as a result in your next life when you had a dire need for it, someone did something extremely kind for you.

Indefinitely Effective Karma

There is another type of karma called indefinite karma, which can also be known as defunct or ineffective karma. This karma does not take place in the next life, but rather it takes place at any time in your lifetimes until you attain nirvana.

Defunct or Ineffective Karma

When karma does not operate in this life at all, it is called defunct or ineffective karma. This means that it did not serve you in this life to teach you a lesson and therefore it becomes ineffective. You may not know in your next life what it was that caused said karma, so it loses its impact.

Understanding the many varieties of karma can allow you to understand why certain things may occur in your life and become mindful over their existence. You can begin to recognize areas of your life where ignorance may be taking place and replace that ignorance with awareness and mindfulness, and thus reduce or eliminate your karma. As well, you should understand the importance of death-proximity karma and reproductive karma. These are ones that have a profound impact on your lifetime of karma. Finally, understanding obstructive and destructive karmas are important, too, as they can completely change the way your karma is judged.

Vipaka is the process by which karma comes to maturity and is experienced. It is directly related to karma and is present in every form of karma. When you experience karma, which is inevitable, you will experience vipaka, which is also inevitable. You may experience the vipaka in this lifetime, or you may experience it in a later lifetime if it is defunct or ineffective karma. One way or another, though, you will experience it.

Chapter Summary:

- Karma is a moral law of cause and effect
- Vipaka is the term for when karma matures and the effect is experienced
- There are many different types of karmas which you can be affected by
- You may experience karma from a past life
- Buddhists believe you can control your karma for your next life based on your dying thoughts

Chapter 18: An Hour Of Silence

This mindfulness technique will make you more accustomed with being yourself. In this exercise, the goal is to sit in silence for an hour.

The task may sound easy, but you will be surprised with how many people cannot keep themselves still for one whole hour.

Follow these instructions when doing this exercise:

In one of your rest breaks at work, you should find a place where you can just sit and do nothing. You should let the people around you know that you are meditating and that you should not be disturbed.

While you are in this state, you need to block out the noise around you. It is easier if you are already in a silent place. If your office is near a public library for instance, you can do this activity there.

You may need some way to block out the noise if you are in a noisy environment. Earplugs are the best solution to this problem.

During the activity, you should try to keep your mind still by doing regular breathing patterns and avoiding responding to the noises or moving objects around you.

You should keep your eyes focused on something that is not moving. Because your will be keeping your eyes in this place or object for a long period, it helps I you choose an object with neutral colors. You should choose something with natural colors like brown, green or blue. You should avoid staring at brightly colored objects.

The challenge of this exercise is to keep still in prolonged hours. At some point, you will question why you are wasting your time with this activity. You should not acknowledge such judging thoughts. Instead, aim silence in your own mind.

As you practice doing this activity, you will become more aware of how cluttered your mind is. Unlike in other exercises however, in this mindfulness technique, we do not try to tame the mind. Instead, we let it entertain the thoughts that simultaneously enter your mind.

Your goal with these thoughts is to calm yourself as you entertain them. At the end of each thought process, you should be calm with no strong emotions.

Every now and then, you will find your emotions becoming stirred up. When this happens, you could exercise the breath counting techniques in earlier chapters to return your heart rate back to normal. When you are calm, you should return to the exercise.

You may also experience exhaustion in doing nothing. Our mind has been trained to keep moving and to keep long for things to do. This exercise will teach you to accept that it is sometimes advantageous to spend some time doing nothing.

Some people who do this exercise report feeling rejuvenated and feel more relaxed after doing the activity.

Chapter 19: The Best Way To Use Self-Compassion To Beat Anxiety

Self-compassion is a means of relating to ourselves that is different from what many of us do. This means estimating ourselves not to what we believe or for how we act. Instead, it is about appreciating our own inherent worth, accepting ourselves and fixing ourselves kindly and especially in difficult circumstances.

The idea of self-compassion first originated from the Buddhist Tradition quite a very long time before but just lately Western researchers start to pay more attention to the psychological ability. Since about the start of the century, countless studies have been completed and by now many psychologists know that self-compassion is still a really crucial attitude to get. Particularly for those people who struggle with anxiety or melancholy.

If we need to properly understand what it has to be self-compassionate, additionally it makes sense to turn into science. Researchers who have brought self-compassion into academia say it includes three vital components:

(1) The Initial one is self-kindness. Section of being self-compassionate is treating ourselves with care and understanding. Self-kindness is the reverse of ourselves harshly.

(2) The second person is mindfulness. By now, most of us have likely heard of mindfulness before it's a way of focusing on our own thoughts and feelings without becoming overwhelmed by these.

(3) The third part is exactly what investigators call ordinary humanity which means understanding that each and every one of us is actually incomplete? It's a part of being a man to make some mistakes and feel terrible sometimes.

The reason why self-compassion is strong is that it allows us to tap into our capability to love and benevolence and flip that this benevolence towards ourselves. Here's how Kristin Neff puts it:

Rather than mercilessly judging and familiarizing yourself to a variety of inadequacies or shortcomings, self-compassion means you're kind and understanding when confronted with personal failings.

This attitude does more than just make us feel great. It may have a true impact on our mental health.

When we have been self-compassionate, our mind's care-giving and self-awareness methods trigger and these brain places are significantly important when we wish to soothe stress. That's the reason one of probably the most constant research findings will be the beneficial impact that self-compassion has about both anxiety and depression. Many people however bring quite a lot of skepticism to the table when it has to do with self-compassion. After all, it seems suspiciously much like self-pity and indulgence. That is why it's important to know that research has also discovered a few health benefits:

We procrastinate less. In comparison to use guilt or fear as inspiration, self-compassion is more successful for ourselves to do things we'd prefer to avoid.

We bounce back from collapse. Rather than spending a great deal of energy and time criticizing ourselves for errors, self-compassion assists us to admit our failures without even questioning our basic self-worth.

We are much more receptive to criticism. For exactly the same reason, self-compassion helps us to acknowledge (negative) suggestions and find out from it. The reason for these surprising advantages is that self-compassion lessens the stress that accompanies failure, criticism and procrastination. It's a mindset that gives us a sense of fundamental self-worth and that makes us more resilient to whatever challenge we may face.

The only way to appreciate those benefits though is to actually place self-compassion into actions. With this, we would like to share just a small exercise with you. It features a terrific way to tap into the potential of a self-compassionate attitude. If you're feeling stressed and inclined to criticize yourself, imagine what you'd do if a friend went through a similar experience.

How could you treat this buddy? Would you attempt to give them all the love, care and understanding that you have? Or do you tell them to not whine and possibly even call these names?

As soon as you have a concept, bring the same attitude to yourself. Rather than mumbling cruel words, treat yourself and remind yourself that lots of different people go through similarly challenging encounters.

What's left? To state is that putting this into action on a daily basis might be hard. That is because self-compassion isn't our default option. When anxiety hits and adrenaline rushes throughout our entire body, we're inclined to revert to older patterns of self-criticism. But the more you exercise this compassionate self-talk the more readily it will come for you. It might take time but you may trust it will earn a permanent positive difference.

How to live your truth? Identifying your values and mastering mindful living

Do you know what the most common sorrow people express in their deathbed is? It is "I wish I had the guts to live a life true to myself, not the lifetime others expected for me."

This blog post is about how not to have this regret on your own sanity.

So, what stops people from living a life that's true to them? Two things:

The first thing that prevents people from living a life that's accurate to these is a simple fact they defined or obtained clear on what is accurate to them. They got clear on which their own deepest values are and what's significant to them.

When we feel of touch with the deepest and truest aspect of ourselves, it is all to normal to encounter just following societal norms and values (that are often very different from your own) or people submit to doing exactly what our loved ones want us to perform (often in an effort to get them to like/approve people) instead of what we really wish to do. Sound familiar?

The next thing that prevents people from living their fact is too little awareness, lack of mindfulness. Without mindfulness, we tend to live a lot of our lives 'auto-pilot' and when we are on auto-pilot we frequently fall into conditioned, mechanical patterns of thought and behavior, most of that we didn't knowingly choose and the majority of that was handed down to us out of our culture and up-bringing.

Residing in unawareness similar to this leads to an awareness of discontent and disconnection in ourselves.

Mindfulness means waking up from autopilot as well as connecting deeply with ourselves as well as the own lives of ours. Mindfulness gives us the capacity not just to hear our hearts but also to stay in contact with what is significant to us but additionally it gives us the capability to respond (from our values) and to not respond (from older conditioning).

In other phrases, mindfulness is needed so as to live your values on a daily basis.

What are values and why are they so important?

All of us have values; they are as much a part of us as our blood types or our genetic makeup. They're rather unique to us since our individual thumb-prints. Our core values decide what's vital and meaningful to us.

Values are who you're in your own deepest nature not that which you feel you should be to be able to match. They are similar to a compass that points us to our "true north".

When the way you think, talk and behave match your values, life feels very good that you feel complete, content in your power. However, when these don't align with your own values then matters feel wrong. Life feels uneasy. You feel out of touch, discontented, nervous and unhappy.

As you can see in the number one sorrow of this dying, there's a steep price to pay for not living in accordance with what is true to you. If life feels 'wrong' many men and women try to fill through outside pleasuring or they may try numbing or deflecting by maintaining busy but before you return to live your truth, before you come back to this inner homeostasis of balance and simplicity, those efforts to fix objects liberally will likely be futile.

That is why making a conscious attempt to identify and live your values is so incredibly important. Here is an easy six-step procedure to assist you identify your own core values.

How to discover your core values in six simple steps?

STEP 1: EXPLORE

Let's start of having a workout to help you clearly identify your core values. Grab a pen and paper or perhaps it's possible to opt to take notes on your computer or device.

Can you recall a time where you felt completely yourself? A peak moment of life when you're in your element, when all felt aligned? A moment when you felt satisfied and happy? Take some time to remember this peak moment. When you're ready, take a few notes explaining this peak moment in some detail.

For example:

At a four-day retreat, its members (there were about 40 of them together) were making a 'final ring' because the spill was drawing to a close. As people started to share one, they really opened their hearts and shared quite intimate stories, spoke of private discoveries and profound insights into the human state. There was a real sense of tenderness, love and camaraderie within the room. There were tears of laughter and tears of joy; they all ended up crying together. It felt so intimate, real and deeply connecting. They felt like they were doing what had to do.

As soon as you've composed down a summit experience of your own.

STEP 2: EXTRACT

Now you've got your peak experience composed, think of what values were being voiced and felt at that moment. What was significant to you personally about this? Second that made it so special?

From the moment I described above, I can extract which I value:

-Appreciate and connection

-Working with individuals to help them suffer less and be happier (contribution).

-Being open, authentic and vulnerable.

-Feelings of courage and strength.

-Vitality; a profound sense of aliveness.

So now jot down a few things from your peak moment. Got them?

STEP 3: CHOOSE

Choose one or perhaps 2 values that you have recognized as the majority of crucial for you. Write them down in the paper of yours. Out of my five values identified above, I feel 'contribution' would be the one which is most significant to me in my entire life. A close second is 'love'.

STEP 4: DEFINE

Now write a bit about what your preferred value (or values) way to you. Various words mean different things to different people, so it is important to define exactly what this value means to you in your lifetime.

To me contribution essentially means that I'm being kind and caring. I'm expressing the love in my heart. I am helping the world to be peaceful, joyful, healthy and in harmony. The contribution is an external flow from my innate feelings of love towards life. The worth of 'love' is very closely related but subtly different to me personally. Enjoy as stated above means to me individually I'm feeling a deep feeling of connection with a different actually being with life in this moment.

Write what your values mean to you personally.

STEP 5: NAME

Opt for a value title that feels right to you. As I said, different words can mean various things for people; therefore it is important to specify how this word is significant to you.

For Instance, the term contribution to me is only meaningful if I'm really expressing my innate love for life.

I would not feel I was expressing my value of contribution if I had been doing someone a favor, for example; performing it begrudgingly. For me, it always has to have genuine loving energy supporting it. Contribution to me personally is active. Another word for contribution, at the way I mean, might be 'kindness'. In fact, I feel that word matches better for me I am going to name this worth 'kindness'.

Additionally perhaps to somebody else 'adore' would mean romantic love also it might mean talking and acting in certain ways. My private significance of love means to me that I am experiencing and expressing feelings of connection and familiarity with a being or with lifetime. So 'love' is my next value name.

What are yours? Jot them down.

STEP 6: REPEAT AS WELL AS REVEAL YOUR CORE VALUES

Now that you've got one or two values now you can repeat steps 1 to 5 until you've got a pair of 5 to seven values. We predict this set of core values. You might see that the exact ones coming up again and again and that's fine. See, however, if you're able to learn more about the brand new ones which appear as you go through the steps again until you have your heart 5 to 7.

The difference between values and goals

There is an important distinction that has to be created between goals and values.

Values provide a deep awareness of continuing leadership for our lives that don't end in themselves. Goals are things that we wish to reach or do, they often end up in themselves. Values always exist in the current moment; they can be drawn at any given instant. Goals have been in the future.

Values aren't rules or commandments.

Some spiritual traditions tell people what they need to value and how they ought to act but that's not what we are speaking about here. Values how we talk of it are publicly chosen by you. Your accurate values aren't levied on you from outside resources. They come from listening to a heart and tuning in to what matters the most to you.

In order to live a life that is authentic to you, you ought to be willing to be entirely honest with yourself about what you appreciate most in life.

Values are maybe not rules or commandments and they're best held gently. They do not have to be static or rigid. Values are going to take brand new types and change and improve over time.

Chapter 20: Walking Meditation

Until now, we have concentrated on meditations that require very little movement. In fact, you have been instructed to sit quietly in a place that you are not likely to be disturbed. Walking meditation is also known as moving meditation and is a form of mindful walking.

This type of meditation requires more interaction between the mind and the body and between the body and its environment. For some, this is the type of meditation is easier, for they can bring the awareness of the movement into the body part that is affected.

There are other types of moving meditation, such as dancing, yoga, and even sports activities. But, one of the most useful and grounding ways is the practice of walking meditation. It is simple and universal. It can help develop a sense of calm, a sense of being connected, and a sense of body awareness.

It can be practiced on a regular basis and can be combined with other forms of sitting meditation if you wish. It can be practiced at any time of the day, after work, or on a day off. The true art of walking meditation is to be aware as you are walking. The natural movement associated with walking can cultivate mindfulness a sense of wakeful presence.

Just as we learned with the eating meditation, just about any activity can be turned into meditation as long as we are mindful and in the moment. It takes some practice to be able to do this, and you must set aside time and employ a bit of patience to make it work.

To practice, first, select a quiet place where you can walk back and forth comfortably. In can be inside or out, just big enough to get ten to thirty paces in length. Begin by standing at one of these walking paths with your feet firmly planted on the ground. You can wear shoes or go barefoot, depending on the weather and your preference. Keep your hands resting easily by your side. Open your sense to see and feel the surroundings. After a minute or so, bring your attention back to the present and focus on your body. Center yourself and feel how your body is standing on the earth. Feel the pressure of your weight on the bottoms of your feet and all the other natural sensations of just standing still in one place. Let yourself be present in the moment and alert.

The theory behind this walking meditation is that we do things like walking, chores and other daily tasks we do on autopilot. We walk mainly to go from point A to point B to finish a task or the like. Walking meditation is meant to walk slowly, taking small steps and focusing your mental awareness on each step and how each step affects you and your body. You bring your focused attention onto the heel, arch, ball, and toes of your feet, feeling each area as they hit the ground.

In many retreats, the course will include mindful walking meditation between sessions of seated meditation. The theory behind this is that the seated meditation may impair the circulation to the lower extremities and walking will increase the blood back to your feet and legs.

It recommended that you begin slowly and that you walk along the same path every time. The purpose behind this is that you want to keep distractions as low as possible, so by walking the same path, you will not be tempted to explore new sights, marvel at the new thing you just saw or worrying about getting lost. Mind wandering is counterproductive to the mind-training aspects of this exercise.

Walking only short and familiar paths break up the session with brief stops. In those turnaround moments, you have a natural choice to check to see if your mind has wandered. There are recommendations that walking meditations should have at least two turnaround points.

Walk back and forth for ten minutes or longer if you desire. As with the other meditations, you will find that your mind does wander away to other topics. When this happens, acknowledge where it went, then go back to the feeling of your foot hitting the ground with the next. This may have to be repeated many times. Whether you have wandered for a short period of time or longer, it doesn't matter. Simply acknowledge it and get back on track.

Use the walking meditation to calm and collect yourself and to live more wakefully in your body. Practice at home first. You can then extend your mindful walking in an informal way when you go shopping, whenever you walk down the street or walk to or from your car. You can learn to enjoy walking for its own sake instead of the usual planning and thinking and, in this simple way, begin to be truly present, to bring your body, heart, and mind together as you move through your life.

Benefits of Walking Meditation

Walking meditation works extremely well when combined with the other seated meditations mentioned so far. You can do this walking meditation alone, but it is rarely a stand-alone practice. The main reason for this that meditations which focus on body consciousness are often decreased. Walking meditations is a challenge simply because of the distractions that can occur when walking.

However, walking meditation can have the same benefits as other meditation, such as increased concentration, increased focus, decreased stress, and prolonged attention. Here are some other benefits that you may receive from walking meditation.

Dignity and confidence: Mindfulness is filled with dignity since we live in a place of present moment awareness. Our actions become more gentle, respectful and dignified. We don't focus on the bad things of ourselves and we don't overreact, living in a more balanced state.

Intentional Living: Often times, when we are anxious, we don't know what to do next. We are impatient to the extreme and we find ourselves looking for more.

Living mindfully, including walking meditation, can be a challenge since the intention of this practice is not to really get anywhere. Instead, it is the walking that is important. This, in turn, fosters a sense of living intentionally, moving intentionally and using deliberate actions.

Personal responsibility: There are many sayings about journeys. "Walk a mile in someone else's shoes", "You alone must walk your path" are just two that comes to mind. The path we are talking about here is the path of personal growth and development. When your mind is in the walking meditation focus, a natural sense of inner resourcefulness comes in, and you can be inspired to be stronger, more confident and have more personal responsibility.

Increased Concentration: In this walking meditation, your mind is trained to disregard most of the external distractions. This is especially true if you practice outside where the sound of other people, traffic, nature or other animals can affect your thoughts.

Relaxed concentration helps you to move deliberately, gracefully, mindfully and also increases your ability to focus without straining the nerves or increasing stress and tension.

Better Moods: Endorphins, or the hormones which are released naturally during activity, including serotonin, helps to elevate your mood, decrease stress, decrease or increase your appetite and help to support cognitive functions.

Mind and Body Connection: Being aware of certain parts of your body when walking gives you a feeling of knowing what your body is doing at a specific second in time.

It helps with balance as well, since you are concentrating on where to place your foot next rather than just blindly stumbling along the path you've chosen.

Deeper Connection to Nature and Community: Outdoor walking is wonderful to observe and connect with nature. Spending time outdoors in a meaningful exercise can be healing to both your body and your soul.

Conclusion

Thank you again for downloading this book!

I hope this book was able to help you to jumpstart your meditation practice.

The next step is to keep doing the steps and techniques that are contained in this book. Remember that mindfulness is not something that you can master in just a couple of weeks. So, if you have to be patient with yourself. Do not give up and just keep on practicing. Soon enough, you'll reap the full benefits of your mindfulness practice. You'll have less stress and worries and the quality of your life will significantly improve. Once you have mastered your mindfulness practice, don't forget to share it with others.

Thank you and good luck!

www.ingramcontent.com/pod-product-compliance
Lightning Source LLC
Chambersburg PA
CBHW072002070526
44583CB00015B/1297